eat.shop london

**first edition : researched, photographed and written by
caroline loncq**

cabazon books : 2008

table of contents

eat

shop

caroline's notes on london

when kaie approached me to author *eat.shop london* i was thrilled. i'm an actress by trade and a mum by good fortune and here was a chance to do something completely different—to eat and be paid for it, to take pictures for work instead of just for fun and to shop with a higher intent. the perfect job for the winter, i thought. so, has it delivered? well, i can tell you it has been a revelation, a huge learning curve and in the process i've rediscovered my own city, a perk which I really wasn't expecting.

certain friends turned out to be invaluable as they sat round the kitchen table expounding on their latest discoveries: matt the assistant director who loves his belly and al "the fire", a photographer and chef manqué, who loves to wine and dine; hege, the events manager for *fifteen*, jamie oliver's restaurant, who loves to eat as much as i do; and spike, her man, who teaches people how to run bars as well as he did. for the record i was born in london and have lived most of my life here, with occasional extended excursions in the states and elsewhere.

london. to me it means freedom: you can be who you are and live as you choose. i love the villages, the green spaces, the markets, the hum of creativity. i always feel a little sorry for tourists in london because so much is hidden here and it will remain that way if the corporate tourist trail is adhered to. i hope this book helps you get past the obvious to the more interesting, whether you're visiting or you live here. if you don't know london, it's imperative to get a good map book to accompany using the maps in this book, which are meant as a snapshot of an area. i'd suggest *the a-z london mini street atlas* or *the a-z london central area notebook*—they are great if you're new to the city and want to wander, always my favourite way to discover anywhere.

i have lived south, north, west and now east in this city—london is huge, geographically and culturally. *eat.shop london* is in no way comprehensive, neither in terms of geography, nor culture. if it was, you'd need a much bigger handbag. like a hummingbird let loose in a vast, beautiful garden and told she can only taste a handful of flowers—i had to be picky. i buzzed east a great deal, partly because, with it's more affordable rents and huge artistic community, there's a wealth of people doing their creative thing in an uncompromised way, making for some of most original, authentic and eclectic small businesses in the city. believe me, i went all over in search of *eat.shop* treats, but the east end blooms smelled sweetest.

for online maps, go to : http://maps.eatshopguides.com/london

caroline loncq
caroline@eatshopguides.com

algerian coffee stores

soho coffee and tea shop

52 old compton street, w1d 4pb. between dean and wardour streets
northern / piccadilly : leicester square <or> central / northern : tottenham court road
020 7437 2480 www.algcoffee.co.uk
mon - wed 9a - 7p thu - fri 9a - 9p sat 9a - 8p

opened in 1887. owner: paul crocetta
$ - $$: all major credit cards accepted
dry goods

soho > **e01**

Soho has its treasures and this is one. Word is that this area is named after the hunting cry "So-ho!" ("There goes the fox!") which, since this area used to be Henry VIII's park for the Palace of Whitehall, makes sense. The man hunted everything that moved, including wives. Don't shout the hunting cry on old Compton Street these days unless you want some action. But do seek out the *Algerian Coffee Stores*. You will rub shoulders with old Chinese ladies as well as coffee buffs, all here in search of the many and varied bean-and-leaf based beverages... as well as teapots that actually pour.

---

imbibe / devour:
119 types of coffee beans ground to order
coffee and teapots in every shape & size
"artistic" tea balls of flower tea
min pu-er two cha birds nest tea
london pottery teapots
xocolata pedra spanish drinking chocolate
calabrian chocolate-covered figs stuffed
  with walnut

andrew edmunds

fine dining with old-school charm
46 lexington street, w1f 0lw. at beak street
central / bakerloo / victoria : oxford circus 020 7437 5708
lunch mon - fri 12.30 - 3p sat - sun 1 - 3.30p
dinner mon - sat 6 - 10.45p sun 6 - 10.30p

opened in 1985. owner: andrew edmunds chef: rebecca st. john cooper
$$ - $$$: mc. visa
lunch. dinner. reservations recommended

soho > e02

I've always thought of *Andrew Edmunds* as the perfect grown-up seduction venue. By grown-up, I'm talking a daily changing menu of great seasonal food, fine wines and exquisite flowers rather than footsie under the table. Though, hey, who am I to ban footsie? Turn off your mobile phone (obligatory), half close your eyes and you're in one of the eighteenth-century satirical prints that Andrew deals from his shop next door. Remember though, you'll need to book here as it's a small place, though in my opinion, perfectly formed.

imbibe / devour:
pol roger white foil nv by the glass
kingston black apple aperitif
chicken liver parfait, onion marmalade,
  cornichons & toast
rump of herdwick lamb with gratin dauphinoise
pearl barley pilaf with feta, roast pumpkin,
  spinach & chestnuts
sticky toffee pudding with ice cream

barrafina

perfect soho tapas

54 frith street, w1d 4sl. between old compton and bateman streets
central / northern : tottenham court road
020 7813 8016 www.barrafina.co.uk
mon - sat noon - 3p 5 - 11p

opened in 2007. owners: sam and edddie hart chef: niveas barragan
$$: all major credit cards accepted
lunch. dinner. full bar. first come, first served

soho > e03

Do I have MTV tastebuds, always hopping on to the next flavour? Or is it more that I can justify a couple of tapas and a glass of something at any time of day or night? The latter comes in handy on this job as this *eat.shop* research is exhausting stuff. No, really, it is. So thank heaven that London is in the throes of a tapas revolution. The Hart brothers already own the well respected tapas spot *Fino*, and I think of *Barrafina* as the gorgeous younger brother, more angular and drop-dead good-looking. Arrive early and enjoy his undivided attention before the Soho crowd crashes your hot date.

imbibe / devour:
great selection of spanish wines
belu sparkling water
caperberries
grilled quail with al-i-oli
chickpeas, spinach & bacon
chorizo, potatoes & watercress
octopus with capers
fig salad

bistrotheque

hidden restaurant and cocktail bar

23 - 27 wadeson street, e2 9dr. between cambridge heath road and mowlem street
central : bethnal green
020 8983 7900 www.bistrotheque.com
mon - fri 6 - 10.30p sat - sun 11a - 4p 6 - 11p (see bar hours online)

opened in 2004. owners: pablo flack and david waddington
$$ - $$$: all major credit cards accepted
brunch. lunch. dinner. cabaret bar
reservations recommended

hackney > 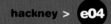 **e04**

If you're into modern art, you'll be making a beeline for the gallery spaces on Vyner Street, round the corner from this chic eatery. Here's my thinking: after art, come cocktails. Then dinner. But be warned: *Bistrotheque* is hidden, so unmarked that you'll need the exact address. Once here, you'll find that David and Pablo have made warehouse chic welcoming. It feels like *Bistrotheque* takes food seriously but life itself with a pinch of salt. Three times a week there's alternative cabaret in the separate downstairs space, and weekend brunches are just as they should be.

imbibe / devour:
champagne cocktail
pisco sour cocktail
grilled seabass with seared queen scallops
sauté of wild mushrooms & herbs
honey-glazed lamb shank & roast carrots
roast butternut squash & sage risotto
chocolate & almond cake
bakewell tart

el vergel

chilean café

8 lant street, se1 1qr. between borough high street and toulmin street
northern : borough
020 7357 0057 www.elvergel.co.uk
mon - fri 8a - 3p sat 10.30a - 3p

opened in 1993. owners: stella de garcia and kiko sanhueza
$: cash
breakfast. brunch. lunch. wine / beer only. first come, first served

borough >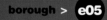

As soon as I got this gig, I made a list. The first of so, so many. On that first list I noted "Chilean café, Lant Street." A few years ago, I recorded a book for the disabled at a recording studio across the road. *Bridget Jones Diary*, since you ask. Oh, the joy when I discovered *El Vergel* at lunchtime, which is tucked away on a side street. It amazes me that so many of my friends know about this great little Chilean joint. How did they all find it? Good news travels fast, obviously.

imbibe / devour:
innocent smoothies
chilean wine
empanadas filled with cheese, spinach or meat
guacamole
churrasco queso (chilean bread filled with
    rump steak, melted cheese & tomatoes)
green bean tortilla salad
cheesecake

eyre brothers

gorgeous iberian cuisine

70 leonard st., ec2a 4qx. between paul and ravey streets. northern : old street <or>
central : bethnal green <or> circle / hammersmith & city / metropolitan : liverpool street
020 7613 5346 www.eyrebrothers.co.uk
mon - fri noon - 3p 6.30 - 10.45p sat 6.30 - 10.45p

opened in 2000. owners: steve and ben chesterfield chefs: david eyre with joao cleto
$$$: all major credit cards accepted
lunch. dinner. full bar. reservations recommended

shoreditch > **e06**

I've answered *Eyre Brothers* to "what's your favourite restaurant?" for so long I almost wondered if it was still true. Then I went to take pictures, tucked into a corner of David's kitchen, and I fell in love all over again. The man's an artist. I felt like I wanted to run away and join the culinary circus. A bit of background: David was the original chef at *The Eagle*, that mother of all gastropubs. Then, for a while, he catered out of his superior sandwich shop. And now he and Robert, the brothers Eyre, have made this place just for me. I share it with you.

---

imbibe / devour:
04 'cal pla' mas d'en compte
bodega de camilo castilla 'capricho de goya'
rabbit & olive terrine with red onion salad
morcilla with fried arrocina beans,
  turnip greens & sherry vinegar
grilled whole dorada with escabeche of
  aromatic vegetables
quince tarte tatin with ginger ice cream

fernandez and wells

soho's premier deli and café

43 lexington street, w1f 9al. between beak and broadwick streets
bakerloo / central / victoria : oxford circus
020 7734 1546 www.fernandezandwells.com
deli mon - fri 11a - 9p sat noon - 9p café mon - fri 8a - 7p sat 9a - 7p

opened in 2007. owners: jorge fernandez and rick wells
$ - $$: mc. visa
breakfast. brunch. lunch. first come, first served

soho > e07

They're called "Food and Wine Bar" and "Coffee Bar." I call them fantastic. I speak of the two parts of the *Fernandez and Wells* show, which are on either side of the corner of Beak and Lexington. Rick and Jorge did that give-up-the-day-job-and-do-what-you-really-want-to-thing. Their ideal places turn out to be ours too. Here you can eat, take your lunch back to the office, have a meeting over coffee or buy your dinner to take home. Soho eats better now thanks to these guys.

imbibe / devour:
chegworth valley apple & raspberry juice
espresso
jamon iberico de berlotta
black pudding & egg in a bun
butternut squash, goats cheese & sage quiche
valrhona chocolate mousse tart with pears
portuguese biscuits with fennel seeds
sicilian lemon cheesecake

fika

swedish food and coffee

161a brick lane, e1 6sb. between bethnal green road and bacon street
northern : old street <or> central : bethnal green <or>
central / circle / hammersmith & city / metropolitan : liverpool street
020 7613 2013 www.fikalondon.com
mon - fri noon - 11p sat - sun 11a - 11p

opened in 2007. owner: sadaf malik
$$: cash
lunch. dinner. coffee / tea. wine / beer only
reservations accepted for parties of four or more

brick lane > **e08**

I passed *Fika* as they were fitting it out before opening and noted the attention to detail being given. My restaurant nose twitched, and I made a mental note to come back. Sure enough, Sadaf (Swedish mother, Asian father) has created a little gem here. *Fika's* witty and welcoming, and the short menu holds your hand and leads you to the Swedish classics, albeit some with a twist. I dropped in here with a friend for coffee, then we decided to have wine instead, then we ordered snacks, then we went for the mains, and so it went. High praise.

imbibe / devour:
norrlands guld lager
swedish roast coffee
gravad lax with dill sauce
three sorters sill (three varieties of pickled herring)
traditional plankstek
lax planka
vegi planka
daim kaka with ice cream

flat white

kiwi coffee shop

17 berwick street, w1f 0pt. between broadwick and peter streets
bakerloo / piccadilly : piccadilly circus <or> bakerloo / central / victoria : oxford circus
020 7734 0370 www.flat-white.co.uk
mon - fri 8a - 7p sat - sun 9a - 6p

opened in 2005. owner: cameron mcclure
$ - $$: cash
breakfast. brunch. lunch. coffee / tea. gallery. first come, first served

soho > **e09**

It's lovely here at *Flat White*, very mellow in spite of the vast quantities of caffeine being drunk by discerning Soho bods and ex-pat antipodeans. These kiwis are fanatical about caffeine. They put the Seattle coffee-heads to shame. Cameron explains it as a kind of "men and sheds" thing. New Zealanders all have their own coffee roasters, you see. The kiwi next to me ordered a triple shot flat white. "Are you mad?" I asked him. "Nah," said he, "it's just that the coffee is so weak in London, I stock up when I get in here, eh." Said he. *Flat White* is full of "eh", by the way. It's a kiwi thing.

imbibe / devour:
flat white
monmouth coffee espresso blend beans
chinotto
citron pressé
organic herbal teas
bacon & halloumi cheese bagel
salad niçoise
croissants

flat white noun / *Austral flaat whyette* / NZ *flet wyte*/
1 An antipodean style coffee which is served as a strong shot of espresso served in a small cup with textured milk; a damn good strong coffee.
2 Lat (DMS) 51° 30'0N Long (DMS) 0° 7'0W

frizzante

bustling italian cantina nestled in a farm in the city

hackney city farm. 1a goldsmith's row, e2 8qa. corner of hackney road

northern : old street <or> central : bethnal green <or>

circle / hammersmith & city / metropolitan : liverpool street

020 7645 0556 www.frizzanteltd.co.uk (see website for second location)

tue - sun 9a - 4p

opened in 2002. owners / chefs: eddy ambrosi, armando varlotta and mauro tesseri

$ - $$: all major credit cards accepted

breakfast. brunch. lunch. first come, first served

border between columbia road and broadway market > e10

Some places can just absorb kid mayhem without it impinging in any way on the foodie experience. *Frizzante* is one of these places. I give thanks that these three Italian chefs broke free from the restaurant kitchen in which they met and that this is what they wanted to do. Oh, and that I can walk here in twenty minutes. Also, that the farm is so lovely, with pottery classes and a newly built straw bale house as well as Larry the donkey. That's a lot of thanks. I do have friends without kids who come here just for the food, so fear not, grown-ups. It works for you, too.

imbibe / devour:
organic elderfloser presse
daioni chocolate milk
big farm breakfast or veggie breakfast
butternut squash risotto
poussin
aubergine parmigiana
home made ice cream
really good freshly baked cake every day

gastro

french brasserie

63 - 67 venn street, sw4 0bd. between bromell's road and clapham high street

northern : clapham common

020 7627 0222

mon - sun 8a - noon

opened in 1994. owners: bertrand le net and roger rolland chef: paul tworek

$$: mc. visa

breakfast. brunch. lunch. dinner. full bar. reservations recommended

clapham >

Ooh la la, *Gastro* is so French it warms the heart. Well, I'm half French, so it warms mine, and I think *Gastro* will thaw the Anglo-Saxon heart too. At lunchtime they do an express menu with no choice, just an entrée and a plat for a fixed, very reasonable, price. In the evening it's à la carte and just what you'd expect from your good local bistro in France. Across the road is the Clapham Picture House, so an early movie followed by a romantic dinner might be just the thing, *n'est ce pas*? Or, if you're *tout seul*, an arthouse flick followed by a romantic dinner for just you. Go on, treat yourself.

imbibe / devour:
breton cider
french wines
langoustines
salade maraichère au chevre chaud
monsieur le tourteau (whole cornish crab)
entrecote avec frites
foie de veau à la lyonnaise
tarte tatin

great queen street

bustling british restaurant

32 great queen street, w2cb 5aa. between drury lane and kingsway
central / piccadilly : holborn <or> piccadilly : covent garden
020 7242 0622
mon 6 - 10.30p tue - sat noon - 2.30p 6 - 10.30p

opened in 2007. owners: michael belben, jonathon jones and rob shaw
chef / owner: tom norrington-davies
$$: mc. visa
lunch. dinner. full bar. reservations recommended

covent garden > **e12**

Michael Belben set up *the* original gastropub *The Eagle* with David Eyre (as in *Eyre Brothers*). Plus the owners here also have *The Anchor and Hope* in The Cut. Good omens indeed. And so it came to pass that *Great Queen Street* is one of those buzzy, foodie places where you will want to squeeze onto the bar if there isn't a table, just so you can eat whatever Tom puts on the day's menu. There's a new renaissance of British cooking in London (what, you haven't heard?) and this is the perfect place to ride that culinary wave.

imbibe / devour:
purity brewery ale
bloody mary
potted shrimps
beetroot & cured anchovy salad
rabbit lasagne
lamb burger
wild duck, red cabbage & pickled walnuts
plum & almond tart

green & red

mexican cantina and tequila bar

51 bethnal green road, e1 6la. at redchurch street
northern : old street <or>
circle / central / hammersmith & city / metropolitan : liverpool street
020 7749 9670 www.greenred.co.uk
mon - sun 6 - 11p bar : sun - thu 6 - midnight sat - sun 6 - 1a

opened in 2005. owners: will beckett, henry bessant, huw gott and dre masso
$$: all major credit cards accepted
dinner. full bar. reservations recommended

brick lane > **e13**

Green & Red is as much a temple to tequila as it is to food. But hey, the food is tasty and well thought out—and I do love tequila, so here it is. I checked this place out on a Wednesday when the downstairs bar wasn't open, and the restaurant was relatively calm and intimate, though I suspect the weekends are much more lively. I give you this sequence that I discovered in NYC and works well for me: food, tequila, dance, tequila, dance. Repeat as necessary. The dancing is not obligatory but stops the hangover. Trust me.

imbibe / *devour:*
mexican beer
205 different tequilas
yam bean, cucumber & peanut salad
cerviche de pulpo (octopus)
charales (whitebait)
pork belly with refried beans & fresh tortillas
sides of black beans, guacamole & salsas
churros con chocolate

green valley

lebanese food emporium
36 - 37 upper berkeley street, w1h 5qe. between edgware road and seymour place
central : marble arch
020 7402 7385
mon - sun 8a - midnight

opened in 1986. owner: mrs. beany
$ - $$: mc. visa
grocery

marylebone > **e14**

Thank you, Kaie for sending me out onto the streets of London to find treasures like *Green Valley*. When the sun comes out (it's January as I write this) I shall go to *Green Valley* and collect the ingredients for a sensational picnic and then wander into Hyde Park, stroll to the Serpentine Gallery, settle down in Kensington Gardens and feast on all the delicious Lebanese dainties I have gathered. I'm salivating already. Since *Green Valley* has everything from items baked fresh from the open-fronted oven to a sweets counter bulging with delights, my picnic shall not want.

imbibe / devour:
lebanese "sandwiches"
many, many meze
a dozen varieties of dates
lebanese olives
more nougats than you knew existed
birds nest pistachio sweet pastries
turkish delight
za'atar & sumac

jones dairy

unique grocery and café

23 ezra street, e2 7rh. corner of horatio street
northern : old street <or> central : bethnal green <or>
central / circle / hammersmith & city / metropolitan : liverpool street
020 7739 5372 www.jonesdairy.co.uk
fri - sat 8a - 1p sun 9a - 2p café: fri - sun 9a - 3p oyster pitstop: sun 11a -2p

opened in 1981. owner: robin whaite chef: abigail sinclair
$ - $$: all major credit cards accepted
breakfast. brunch. first come, first served

columbia road > **e15**

100 years ago, Mr. Jones kept six dairy cows here and delivered the milk to locals by pony power. Every six months he'd walk the cows back to Wales (that's some distance) and return with six more. Now, on Fridays and Saturdays you can eat at a table in the whitewashed *Jones Dairy* and buy lovely groceries in the shop next door. On Sundays the table, and usually the soup, is gone and then it's all coffee and beigels (the East End spelling of bagel) for the flower market crowd with the Sunday Oyster Pitstop keeping the London tradition of oysters as street food alive. Foodie heaven.

imbibe / devour:
hot chocolate
fresh organic lemon squash
smoked salmon & cream cheese beigel
almond croissant
abigail's wonderful puy lentil with scallop soup
welsh dry cure bacon from carmathon
echiré french farmhouse butter
selection of english cheeses

la fromagerie

the ultimate cheese shop and tasting café

2 - 4 moxon street, w1u 4ew. between cramer and marylebone high street
central / jubilee : bond street <or>
bakerloo / circle / hammersmith & city / jubilee / metropolitan : baker street
020 7935 0341 www.lafromagerie.co.uk
mon 10.30a - 7.30p tue - fri 8a - 7.30p sat 9a - 7p sun 10a - 6p

opened in 2002. owner: patricia michelson
$$: all major credit cards accepted
breakfast. brunch. lunch. wine / beer only. grocery. first come, first served

marylebone > **e16**

When I arrived at *La Fromagerie* I fell in love. Foodie love. A very special kind of infatuation, as I think you know. I took more pictures here than is decent. It was an exquisite affair and I shall be taking it up again at the earliest possible opportunity, inhaling the amazing aromas in the temperature-controlled cheese room and fondling the fig balls. As for eating on site, there's a tasting café, where you can rest and have lunch, and they do special events and tastings every month. With the great *Ginger Pig* butcher next door, Moxon Street can now fill your larder and fridge as well as tum.

imbibe / devour:
extensive range of english & french cheeses
plus some spanish & italian cheeses
bath oliver biscuits
slowly baked fig balls
charcuterie
italian fruit & vegetables
valrhona drinking chocolate
tasting café - menu changes daily

leila's shop

chic food shop with coffee and eats
17 calvert avenue, e2 7jp. corner of arnold circus
northern : old street <or>
central / circle / hammersmith & city / metropolitan: liverpool street
020 7729 9789
thu - sat 10a - 6p sun 10a - 4p

opened in 2002. owner: leila mcalister
$$: all major credit cards accepted
lunch. brunch. coffee / tea. grocery. first come, first served

shoreditch > e17

My Shoreditch friend Brem says he knew it was over when he saw an ad for a "basement loft-style apartment." Yet here, on the edge of the madness, is Arnold Circus, a circular park which lies at the heart of the boundary estate, an 1880s social housing project that still has a strong, mixed community. Leila sees her shop as part community centre, part grocer. She's very into the regeneration of the circus and does cool projects with designers (friendsofarnoldcircus.wordpress.com). And she makes and sells nice things to eat. I like this shop. I like food. I like coffee. What's not to like?

imbibe / devour:
robert wilson ceylon tea
auberge de chassignol sunflower oil
puy lentils from auberge de chassignol
iranian gaz pistacchio nougat
elvas sugar plums
polish platter: sausage, rye bread, egg,
  pickles & horseradish
flowerpower chocolate brownies

little georgia

georgian café

87 goldsmith's row, e2 8qr. at key street
central : bethnal green
020 7739 8154
mon 9a - 6p tue - sun 9a - 9.30p

opened in 2007. owner: tiko tuskadze
$ - $$: mc. visa
breakfast. brunch. lunch. dinner. coffee / tea. unlicensed (byo)
reservations accepted for parties of three or more

broadway market > **e18**

Georgian food... admit it, you're curious. Tiko has been feeding the Broadway market denizens Georgian food for a few years now, and after a forced move we find her in this great little venue. Vegetarians love it here at *Little Georgia*, with the legendary stuffed cheesebread and Russian salads. Diehard carnivores are more than happy, too. It's a place where time stops and you feel like you're on holiday from the outside world. Tiko's natural grace and charm give *Little Georgia* its character and keep it as a firm favourite with the locals, including lucky me.

imbibe / devour:
many different teas
borjoni georgian mineral water
aladzi (georgian banana & apple pancakes)
chizi bizhi (georgian fry-up breakfast)
pilmeni (georgian ravioli)
hachapuri (stuffed cheesebread)
russian salad
borsht

locanda locatelli

tip-top italian restaurant

8 seymour street, w1h 7jz. at berkeley mews
central : marble arch
020 7935 9088 www.locandalocatelli.com
mon - thu noon - 3p 6.45p - 11p fri noon - 3p 6.45 - 11.30p
sat 6.45 - 11.30p sun noon - 3.30p 6.45 - 10.15p

opened in 2002. owner / chef: georgio locatelli
$$$: all major credit cards accepted
lunch. dinner. full bar. reservations recommended

marylebone > **e19**

I never got the baby blues, and for this I credit Georgio Locatelli. When my son Jonjo was four days old, he fell asleep at the perfect hour. I felt great and said, "oh, why not?" and scooped him up. Off we all went to drop in on a friend's surprise birthday gathering, with food by Georgio. I assumed motherhood was always going to be like this, all swanning around feeling glamourous and eating food made by the gods. Ha, ha. If you're coming to London on a trip, book at *Locanda* before you leave home as the Michelin Star and the brilliance of this place keeps 'em coming, as they should.

imbibe / devour:
sensational list of italian wines
 (i counted over 50 barolos)
wild chicory, caper & anchovy salad
malfatti filled with pumpkin in butter & sage
char grilled mackerel in a herb crust
roasted rabbit leg, parma ham & polenta
green tea mousse, pistachio sponge &
 prosecco sorbet
marsala zabaione

macondo

chic spanish, mexican and bolivian hangout
8 & 9 hoxton square, n1 6nu. west side of hoxton square
northern : old
020 7729 1119 www.macondo.co.uk
mon - sun 8a - midnight

opened in 2002. owners: santiago calva and pablo casas
chefs: augustina and maria
$ - $$: mc. visa
breakfast. brunch. lunch. dinner. coffee / tea. full bar
reservations accepted for parties of two or more

shoreditch > **e20**

"I have found a new haunt" were the words I said to Simon, my other half, earlier today. And I meant it. I want to be one of the regulars that Santiago greets so warmly at *Macondo*. Eat, drink coffee, look at the art on the walls, people watch, hang, that's my plan. Sounds good to me. Unbelievably, Santiago and Pablo opened *Macondo* without any restaurant experience but they have the gift, believe me. They have just opened a second *Macondo* in Camden Passage, with a bigger kitchen. Here, it's tiny. Bless *eat.shop* for bringing me to this haven.

imbibe / devour:
homemade lime-aid
pisco sour cocktail
huevos a la mexicana
chorizo tortilla with salad
empanadas
andlucian fabada
galician baked cheesecake
fabulous cakes

maison bertaux

french patisserie and soho institution

28 greek street, w1d 5dq. between old compton street and shaftesbury avenue
northern / piccadilly : leicester square <or> central / northern : tottenham court road
020 7437 6007
mon - sat 9a - 10p sun 9.30a - 7.30p

opened in 1871. owner: michele wade chefs: nabil and george
$$: cash
coffee / tea. treats. first come, first served

soho > e21

Sometimes I yearn for crème patissière with fruit on top and light pastry beneath. On days like these I know where to come. *Maison Bertaux*. I've been coming here since I was a child. Actually, that probably explains the particular peculiar comfort I get from crème patissière. On a sunny day, sitting outside *Maison Bertaux* with a newspaper, a coffee and a sweet thing is one of Soho's top treats. It's the best people-watching venue I know and has a unique theatrical eccentricity about it. *Maison Bertaux* is the bees knees.

imbibe / devour:
pot of earl grey tea
café au lait
fruit tart with crème patissière
macaroons
palmier
fruit cheesecake
éclair au chocolate
broccoli quiche

45

makan café

malaysian café in the heart of portobello

270 portobello rd, w10 5ty
under the westway between cambridge gardens and lancaster road
hammersmith / city : ladbroke grove <or> central / circle / district : notting hill gate
020 8960 5169 www.makancafe.co.uk
mon - sun 11a - 9.30p

opened in 1992. owner / chef: hairani mohamad
$: mc. visa
lunch. dinner. coffee / tea. first come, first served

portobello > 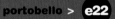

When I lived in Westbourne Grove I had a banana button habit and would cycle to *Makan Café* to get my fix. The banana button is a cross between banana bread and a doughnut, not too sweet, you get my drift? While I was here, I would often pick up my evening dinner as a takeaway for later consumption. Now, when I come back to Portobello, I make a beeline for *Makan Café* as you should too when you're coming to check out Portobello Market. It's a great pit stop in the heart of the action. Top tip: the market is less manic on Fridays than Saturdays.

imbibe / devour:
fresh mint tea
teh tarik (malaysian tea)
sweetcorn bhaji
chicken padang
aubergine sambal
vegetarian laksa
coconut rice
banana buttons

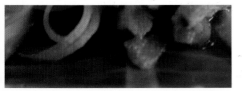

marine ices

italian restaurant and ice cream parlour

8 haverstock hill, nw3 2bl. at adelaide road
northern : chalk farm
020 7482 9003 www.marineices.co.uk
restaurant: tue - fri noon - 3p 6 - 11p sat noon -11p sun noon - 10p
ice cream parlour: tue - sat 11a - 11p sun 11a - 10p

opened in 1931. owners: dante, gino and gaetano mansi
$ - $$: mc. visa
lunch. dinner. treats. wine / beer only. reservations recommended

camden >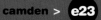

Kids sit up and eat well and babies don't cry here. I don't know why. Like a pair of familiar slippers, the food at *Marine Ices* is simple, traditional and comforting. Like home cooking, but better (sorry, Mum). And then there's the ice cream. It's made here, and it's really good. When I was pregnant, and ice cream became a medical necessity, all roads led here. Detours are still frequent in the summer. A good way to take on the mania of Camden, should you feel the need, would be to start here, then wander down the hill. Or from here you could walk through to Primrose Hill, cone in hand, smile on face.

imbibe / devour:
valverde mineral water
italian wine list
calamari della casa
bruschetta gaetano
linguini alla vongole
pizza menu
fantastic ice creams
sensational sorbets

medcalf

restaurant and bar with an english theme
40 exmouth market, ec1r 4qe. between farringdon road and skinner street
northern : angel <or> circle / hammersmith & city / metropolitan : farringdon
020 7833 3533 www.medcalfbar.co.uk
sun noon - 4p mon - sat noon - 3p 6 -10.30p bar mon - sat 6 - 12.30a

opened in 2003. owners: simon lee and brent unsworth chef: brent taylor
$$: all major credit cards accepted
lunch. dinner. full bar. reservations accepted for parties of four or more

farringdon > e24

My first experience of *Medcalf* ended with me dancing on a table, but that was in the old days when one night a week was turned over to music. These days, food rules the roost, so the djs have given way to a great English seasonal menu. Well, we all have to pretend to grow up sometime. The lovely relaxed ethos hasn't changed though. Here is a place where they won't hurry you away from your lunch table and where regulars drop in for a pint or a coffee in the calm of the afternoon. Sited right next to the wonderful *Moro*, *Medcalf* needs to be excellent to hold its own. So it is, and so it does.

imbibe / devour:
aspalls organic cyder
old world wines
salt cod fishcake with poached egg
organic salmon, swiss chard &
  jerusalem artichoke purée
game pie
bavette steak, chip & horseradish cream
sticky date pudding with toffee sauce

ottolenghi

wonderful food shop

63 ledbury road, w11 2ad. between lonsdale road and westbourne grove
central / circle / district : notting hill gate
020 7727 1121 www.ottolenghi.co.uk (see website for other locations)
mon - fri 8a - 8p sat 8a - 7p sun 8.30a - 6p

opened in 2002. owner: yotam ottolenghi
$$: all major credit cards accepted
breakfast. lunch. dinner. first come, first served

notting hill > e25

There are only ten seats at one communal table at *Ottolenghi*, plus two stools at a counter outside. That's the bad news. The rest is all very good news indeed. It's one of those places where every offering tempts. I even found myself lusting after a raspberry meringue here, and meringues are the devil's food. They have another place in Upper Street—Islington, which has more seating, and is equally fabulous. But this, the original, has a boutique charm which has won me over. At lunchtime you'll be lucky to get a seat but it's worth a wait, believe me.

imbibe / devour:
coffee
croissants
wonderful vegetable salads
superb cold meats
cornbread
flourless chocolate cake
raspberry meringue
white chocolate cheesecake with cranberry

pellicci's

traditional east end caff with knobs on

332 bethnal green road, e2 0ag. between vallance and hague streets

central : bethnal green

020 7739 4873

mon - fri 6.15a - 4.45p sat 6.15a - 4.30p

opened in 1900. owner: nevio pellicci chef: maria pellicci

$: cash

breakfast. brunch. lunch. tea / coffee. first come, first served

bethnal green > 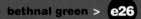 **e26**

Pellicci's: the best caff (as opposed to café) in the universe. Well, in my universe. Priamo and Elide opened it a hundred years ago. Anna will call you "young man/lady" whatever your age and she and Nevio will tempt you with whichever special Mum has cooked that day. Then they will natter to each other in Italian, while having a right banter with all the regulars in English at the same time. It's small and you may be sharing a table, but you'll be part of a very special East End Italian family as soon as you step through the door.

imbibe / devour:
lemon tea
café latte
full breakfast: eggs, bacon, sausage, tomatoes, mushrooms & a fried slice plus bubble & squeak
home-cooked roast beef sandwiches
chicken rusticana
"mum's" jam tart

pinchito

tapas bar

sophia house: 32 featherstone street, ec1y 8qx. between mallow street and city road
northern : old street
020 7490 0121 www.pinchito.co.uk
mon - fri 8a - 11p sat 5 - 11p

opened in 2007. owners: jason fendick, miguel jessen, bruce bartholomew,
emily wheldon and tobias blezquez garcia
$$: all major credit cards accepted
breakfast. brunch. lunch. dinner. coffee / tea. grocery. full bar
reservations accepted for parties of four or more

shoreditch > e27

When I called Hege, who recommended *Pinchito* to me, to check with her the exact address, she said, "I'll meet you there." Then Simon, my man, rocked up, then Spike, her man arrived and I had to bat them, and Jonjo (my little man) off the food so I could take pictures of it. This sums up *Pinchito*. It's relaxed, welcoming and delicious in every way. By the time we'd eaten our meal, I felt like a regular. Plus they do chocolaté con churros, which always seals the deal for me.

imbibe / devour:
moritz beer from barcelona
zoco pacherán navarro (anise & sloe berry drink)
pork belly
octopus with potatoes & chorizo
pimientos de padre hanger steak
champis al ajillo
chocolaté con churros

raoul's

gourmet café and restaurant famed for brunch

105 - 107 talbot road, w11 2at. between ledbury road and powys square
hammersmith / city : westbourne park <or> central / circle / district : notting hill gate
020 7229 2400 www.raoulsgourmet.com
mon - sun 8.30a - 10.15p

opened in 2005. owner: geraldine leventis
$$: all major credit cards accepted
breakfast. brunch. lunch. dinner. coffee / tea. full bar
reservations accepted for parties of four or more

notting hill > **e28**

This is the younger outpost of the original *Raoul's* in Maida Vale. Thank heaven they only have the two eateries, plus a deli across the road in Maida Vale. Much bigger and they'd have fallen foul of the *eat.shop* house rules (no more than three locations, thank you). I've lost count of how many people from the Westside raved about *Raoul's*, but it was the dreamy half-closed expression on my friend Matt's face as he said, "breakfast at *Raoul's*, oh god…" that clinched it. I now know what he meant, and Raoul's is now etched into the foodie map in my head.

imbibe / devour:
berry nice smoothie
milkshakes
full english breakfast with bacon &
   cumberland sausage
grilled kippers & toast
fruit salad, greek yoghurt, honey & nuts
raoul's organic hamburger
toulouse sausages & mash with onion gravy

rochelle canteen

cult canteen

rochelle school at arnold circus, e2 7es. corner of club row

northern : old street <or>

central / circle / hammersmith & city / metropolitan : liverpool street

020 7729 5677 www.arnoldhenderson.com

mon - fri noon - 3p

opened in 2005. owners: melanie arnold and margot henderson

chef: kevin mcfadden

$$ - $$$: mc. visa

lunch. reservations recommended

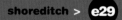

Out of this magical kitchen runs not only a catering company, but also a lunchtime restaurant for the creative types who work in the surrounding converted school buildings, and for those locals who love great food. To get to *Rochelle Canteen*, find the school, press the bell marked "canteen." This is where any association with school food ends. I am salivating as I write this, remembering the beautiful simplicity and exquisite ingredients of my last lunch here. And as a side note, Margot's other half is Fergus Henderson of the legendary *St. John*, which is also not to be missed.

imbibe / devour:
menu changes daily but for example:
    ginger beer
    pg tips tea
    jerusalem artichoke soup
    pheasant pie
roast beetroot & lentils
red cabbage & chestnuts
rhubarb tart

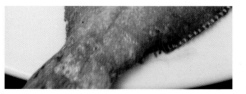

saki

japanese restaurant with cocktail bar

4 west smithfield, ec1a 9jx. between farringdon road and long lane
circle / hammersmith & city / metropolitan : barbican / farringdon
020 7489 7033 www.saki-food.com
mon - fri noon - 2.15p 6.30 - 11p sat 6.30 - 11p

opened in 2006. owner: ayako watanabe chef: hiroyuki saotome
$$ - $$$: all major credit cards accepted
lunch. dinner. grocery. full bar. reservations recommended

farringdon > e30

Saki may be my last great discovery on this *eat.shop* journey. As my deadline approaches, Kaie is breathing down my neck to feature a great Japanese restaurant. Rest easy boss, I've found it. I went to Tokyo a few years ago and was struck when I returned home to London how easy it is here to accept an ersatz Japanese food culture: sushi, sashimi and ramen. Not at *Saki* though. This is contemporary, authentic Japanese food served in a glorious space, complete with wax sculptures and super-gadget loos. They even have a grocery upstairs for your Japanese foodie needs.

imbibe / devour:
honoko cocktail
over 30 different sakes
fois gras & eel spring roll
prawn shinjo ball in yuzu citrus scented soup
saiko miso marinated grilled black cod
rib eye teriyaki
grilled iberico pork with sea salt & black pepper
green tea tiramisu with homemade ice cream

samson miro

fine wine shrine

75 chamberlayne road, nw10 3nd. at station terrace
london overground : kensal rise
020 8962 0275 www.samsonmiro.com
mon - wed noon - 9p thu - sat noon - midnight sun noon - 7p

opened in 2006. owners: samson jesi and mair darda
$ - $$: mc. visa
light dinner. wine only. reservations accepted for parties of six or more

kensal rise > e31

I knew my *eat.shop* eye was really working when I nearly fell off my bike rubbernecking this place. First you have to know that I love wine. I'm half French, so it's a genetic thing. *Samson Miro* is a bar-come-shop specialising in artisan old-world wines from small producers. You won't find these wines anywhere else in the UK and, since it's both a wine merchant and a bar, you can buy a bottle, or five cases, or just have a glass on site. These guys work personally with every producer so they know more than you will ever need to know about each bottle. Passionate wine talk, without pretension.

imbibe / devour:
bergeronneau champagne
selection of bourgogne aligote
glorious range of italian & french wines from
  small vineyards
cold platters of antipasti:
  cured meats, salami, cheeses & ciabatta

65

shipps tearooms

cream tea and cucumber sandwiches

4 park street, se1 9ab. at stoney street
jubilee / northern : london bridge
020 7407 2692 www.shippstearooms.co.uk
wed - thu 10a - 5.30p fri - sat 10a - 6p sun 11a - 6p

opened in 2007. owners: john rich and margaret willis
$ - $$: cash
breakfast. light lunch. tea. treats. reservations accepted for parties of four or more

borough >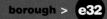

Sandwiched between the two fabulous local institutions *Monmouth Coffee House* and *Neal's Yards Dairy* and opposite Borough Market (all imperative foodie destinations) is the elegant, yet unstuffy *Shipps Tearooms*. I have been known to take tea in the grander London hotels, but from now on, when I get that cream tea urge, I'm going to come here. For one thing, I can buy any of the china, tablecloths or cakestands that catch my fancy; for another I can stock up on my staples of cheese and coffee from the quality purveyors on either side. A lovely one-stop waistline buster.

imbibe / devour:
orange pekoe tea
first flush darjeeling tea
full afternoon tea
cream tea with neal's yard clotted cream &
    miller's bakery scones
anne martin's victoria sponge cake
smoked salmon sandwiches on wholemeal bread
cucumber sandwiches on white bread

spinach & agushi

ghanaian food stand

broadway market, e8 4ph. between dericote and westgate streets
central : bethnal green
020 7254 5333 www.spinachandagushi.co.uk
sun 11a - 4.30p

opened in 2004. owners: adwoa hagen-mensah and lloyd mensah
$: cash
lunch. first come, first served

broadway market > **e33**

I was pleased as punch that Kaie, having eaten here, suggested including this market stall because I have been eating at Adwoa and Lloyd's *Spinach & Agushi* since their first week at the market. My advice: get a coffee from the excellent *Climpson and Sons* just behind, choose your hearty jollof rice and stew combi plus plantain and, if it's summer, head for London fields to picnic. If you choose, you can then abandon your Saturday afternoon to reading the paper with a pint of something from *The Pub on the Park* and half an eye on the cricket which has been played here since 1802.

imbibe / devour:
spinach & agushi (melon seeds) with mushrooms
peanut chicken
beef & pepper stew
bean stew
jollof rice
fried plantains

story deli

glorious redefinition of the pizza place
3 dray walk at the truman brewery. 91 brick lane, e1 6ql. between quaker and hanbury
central / circle / metropolitan / hammersmith & city : liverpool street <or>
district / hammersmith & city : aldgate east
020 7247 3137
mon - fri noon - 4p sat - sun noon - 6p

opened in 2004. owner / chef: lee hollingworth
$ - $$: all major credit cards accepted
lunch. coffee / tea. wine / beer. first come, first served

brick lane > 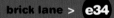 **e34**

My world is a better place for *Story Deli*. The pizzas are extraordinarily light and crisp affairs served on wooden boards at communal tables. Here environmental sustainability is a practical reality rather than a government soundbite. *Story Deli* food is 100% organic. Yes, even the spices. Seats are sustainable cardboard boxes. This is a twenty-first century vision of a better way. Praise be, it's also a delicious one. Lee's partner, Ann, has *Story* (see shop) which makes for a dream marriage of both eat and shop. Hats off to them both.

imbibe / devour:
luscombe organic hot ginger beer
freedom beer
pizza:
   pumpkin, goat cheese & roasted red peppers
   ham & gorgonzola with olives
   chorizo & almond pizza
spinach, borlotti beans & jerusalem artichoke soup
organic ice cream

sweet

boulangerie and patisserie with seating

64 exmouth market, ec1r 4qp. between tysoe street and farringdon road
northern : angel <or> circle / hammersmith & city / metropolitan : farringdon
020 7713 6777 www.sweetdesserts.co.uk
mon - sat 7a - 5.30p sun 8a - 5.30p

opened in 2003. owners: edwin grappy and sebastian wind chef: justice akownah
$ - $$: mc. visa
breakfast. lunch. coffee / tea. treats. first come, first served

exmouth market > e35

Once again, caterers (see *Rochelle Canteen*) open their doors to punters (to you Yanks, this means paying customers) and it pleases me mightily. I have discovered in the course of working on this book, that this practice unites many of my favourite places, both the highbrow and the more rough and ready. I think it's a foodie thing—owners, like the ones at *Sweet*, put food before marketing plans, and they can do that because they already have a good thing going in the kitchen. So I recommend this warm and friendly place as a drop in, take out, snack up venue par excellence. 'Nuff said.

imbibe / devour:
lemon tea
chaya latte
rare breed pork sausage rolls
goats cheese puff with rocket
chorizo pizza
cous cous salad
lemon tart
cherry cheesecake tart

tayyabs

pakistani punjabi cuisine

83 - 89 fieldgate street, e1 1ju. between new road and parfett street
district / east london / hammersmith & city : whitechapel
020 7247 6400 www.tayyabs.co.uk
mon - sun noon - 11.30p

opened in 1975. owner / chef: mohammed tayyab
$ - $$: all major credit cards accepted
lunch. dinner. unlicensed (byo). first come, first served

whitechapel > e36

On a back street in Whitechapel, a five-minute stroll from the bottom of Brick Lane, *Tayyabs* serve sensational curries, sizzling dishes that make me sizzle and a salted lassi that I can still taste if I close my eyes. This place is no longer a secret and in the evenings you'll be faced with a queue, but do it, no question. Or come in the day, as many wise souls do, to savour the fantastic Pakistani dishes in peace. You'll need to bring your alcohol in with you. And your empty stomach. And be prepared to undo that top button on your waistband at the end of your meal.

imbibe / devour:
salted lassi
mango lassi
mixed grill
tandoori lamb chops
karahi tarka dhal
karahi mixed vegetables
tandoori nan
many indian sweets

teasmith

exceptional tea house

6 lamb street, e1 6ea. between commercial and steward streets
central / circle / metropolitan / hammersmith & city : liverpool street
020 7247 1333 www.teasmith.co.uk
mon - sun 11a - 6p

opened in 2006. owner: john kennedy
$ - $$: mc. visa
tea. treats. classes. first come, first served

spitalfields > e37

At my elbow as I type, I have a cup of jasmine tea made with pearls from *Teasmith*. I am now a happy clappy proper tea addict, thanks to John, the tea master, and his team. Unashamed missionaries, they talk openly and with messianic zeal, though not without irony, of brainwashing the customers. In a good way. Here you watch and learn. And drink. It's fun. You can nibble too: chocolates by *William Curley*, chocolate-dipped figs and walnut and miso biscuits. All to enhance your experience of trying new teas. So take a break from the bustle of Spitalfields and enter a world of tea worship.

imbibe / devour:
thistle blossom flower tea
sampler pack of green/white/oolong/puer tea
premium oolong teas from ancient plants
sparrows tongue green tea from korea
xtra old tippy puer matured for 12 years
gyokuro finest japanese green tea
glass infuser mug with ceramic infuser
yixing clay pots

the cinnamon club

upmarket modern indian restaurant

the old westminster library. 30 - 32 great smith street, sw1p 3bu
between victoria and great peter streets
circle / district / jubilee : st. james park <or> westminster
020 7222 2555 www.cinnamonclub.com
mon - fri 7.30 - 9.30a noon - 2.45p 6 - 10.45p sat noon - 2.45p 6 - 10.45p

opened in 2001. owners: martin zapico, mark whitehead, jamie morrison
paul mora, bola lafe and shaun miell chef: vivek singh
$$$: all major credit cards accepted
breakfast. brunch. lunch. dinner. full bar. reservations recommended

westminster > 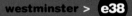 **e38**

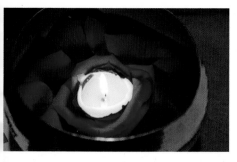

London's love affair with the food of India began in 1809 with Deen Mahomet's Hindustani Coffee House. My love affair with *The Cinnamon Club* began a couple of years ago when friends held their wedding reception here. The. Best. Wedding. Food. Ever. *The Cinnamon Club* is a stone's throw from the Houses of Parliament, so all sorts of interesting people have discovered it. There's a book-lined bar in which the great and good lounge and meet. And then there's the lovely, airy restaurant in which your tastebuds will feel like they have reawakened and have had a morning stretch after a long sleep.

imbibe / devour:
lychee & rose petal martini
king prawn & char-grilled swordfish
roast saddle of oisin red deer with pickling spices
smoked rack of lamb with rajasthani corn sauce
   & pilau rice
tandoor roasted aubergine crush
dark chocolate tart with cumin & buffalo milk
   ice cream

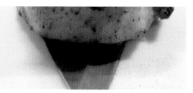

the elk in the woods

cool and comfortable foodie bar

39 camden passage, n1 8ea. between duncan street and charlton place
northern : angel
020.7226.3535 www.the-elk-in-the-woods.co.uk
mon - sat 10.30a - 11p sun 10.30a - 9.30p

opened in 2003. owners: katie rumm and astrid skelly chef: chery-lyn booth
$ - $$: mc. visa
breakfast. brunch. lunch. dinner. full bar. first come, first served

islington > **e39**

I love a place that I can drop into anytime of the day and have, well, whatever is called for at that particular moment, be it breakfast, pancakes, coffee, lunch, dinner or just, in the words of Winnie the Pooh, a little smackerel of something. For Pooh, that always means honey. For me, I think a cocktail and a snack would almost always cover it. *The Elk in the Woods* crew have a sister place in Soho called *Bar Chocolate* so between the two, there is always a leather armchair waiting. *The Elk in the Woods* feels like an open-house private club. Just what the good doctor ordered.

imbibe / devour:
elderflower martini
gin apple smash
mint crusher non-alcoholic cocktail
fennel-roasted pork belly sandwich
braised lamb stew with leeks & haricot beans
salt & pepper calamari with roast chilli
pancakes with baked cinnamon pears, goats
cheese yoghurt & honey

the golden hind

fish and chips

73 marylebone lane, w1u 2pn. between marylebone high street and bulstrode place
central / jubilee : bond street
020 7486 3644
mon - fri noon - 3p 6 - 10p sat 6 - 10p

opened in 1914. owner: tony christou
$: all major credit cards accepted
lunch. dinner. unlicensed (byo). reservations accepted for parties of four or more

marylebone > 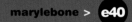 e40

Great fresh fish, light batter, chunky chips, tables and chairs, lovely people, bring your own wine in the evening... hang on, I hear you cry, this is not typical British fish and chips, surely? Well, yes and no. Fish and chips, normally eaten on the street outside the chippie, does one of three things: lines the stomach, satisfies a late night craving or soaks up a hangover. For the full flourescent lighting, eat-outside-the-chippie archetype I go to the one on Berwick Street, but for a more pleasing sit-down experience, with unbeatable fish and chips, *The Golden Hind* is perfection.

imbibe / devour:
tea
orange juice
haddock & chips, mushy peas & pickled onion
cod fishcakes
skate wing
halibut steak
greek salad
spotted dick

HISTORY

1914-1947	Mr. Esposito-Italian
1947-1955	Mr. Morri-Italian
1955-1994	Mr. Schiavetta-Italian
1994-2002	Mr. Stavrothendas-Greek

the royal oak

traditional sunday lunch
73 columbia road, e2 7rg. corner of ezra street
northern : old street <or>
circle / central / hammersmith & city / metropolitan : liverpool street
020 7729 2220 www.royaloaklondon.com
mon 6 - 10p tue - sun noon - 4p 6 - 10p bar noon - 11p

opened in 2005. owners: sarah dewe, neil gregory and naomi rogers
$ - $$: all major credit cards accepted
lunch. dinner. full bar. reservations recommended

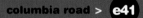

columbia road > e41

This pub's been here for 100 years, but the good food hit the map with the new owners a couple of years ago. Suddenly my foodie pals Baba and Toby were always 'grabbing a bite' at the *Oak*, and I knew something was up. So, if you want upmarket Sunday lunch, go to *Simpson's in The Strand*. If you want gastro heaven book for *The Anchor and Hope* in The Cut. But if you're after really lively, archetypal hearty pub Sunday roast and great Yorkshire pudding in the flower market, come to *The Royal Oak*. Book into the dining room upstairs or pounce on a table in the large downstairs bar.

imbibe / devour:
bloody mary
guinness
fennel, watercress & rocket salad
roast beef with yorkshire pudding
roast lamb
stuffed butternut squash
chips & mayonnaise
apple & rhubarb crumble with cream

treacle

new nostalgia cupcakes

110 - 112 columbia road, e2 7rg. between barnet grove and ravenscroft street

northern : old / central : bethnal green <or>

central / circle / hammersmith & city / metropolitan : liverpool street

020 7729 5657 www.treacleworld.com

sun 9.30a - 3.30p

opened in 2003. owners: tom and bux jacobsson

$ - $$: all major credit cards accepted

treats. tea. first come, first served

columbia road > e42

As I took pictures at *Treacle*, a woman buying an impossibly beautiful cupcake looked over at me with shining eyes and said, "this place makes me feel like a little girl!" And, with a smile, took her "precious" away. So men, unleash your inner little girl—you know you want to; and women, you know the address. You can buy lovely homeware things here too, so I thought about putting this biz on the shop side of this book. But *Treacle* is all nibble, taste, eat. The Sunday flower market is on the street outside which is a riot of colour, and *Treacle* is the icing on the cake.

imbibe / devour:
tea (don't mention the c word here)
old-fashioned lemonade
cupcakes in large, medium &
  unbearably cute tiny sizes:
    traditional vanilla
    luxurious chocolate
    lemon
treaclebocker glory layer cake

verde & co.

delightful food shop

40 brushfield street, e1 6ag. corner of gun street
central / circle / metropolitan / hammersmith & city : liverpool street
020 7247 1924 www.verde-and-company-ltd.co.uk
mon - sun 8.30a - 5p

opened in 2004. owner: harvey cabannis premises owned by: jeanette winterson
$ - $$: all major credit cards accepted
lunch. grocery. coffee / tea. treats. first come, first served

spitalfields > **e43**

In the morning, *Verde & Co.* buzzes with preparation. At lunchtime, a steady stream of discerning wage slaves pick up their pre-booked orders, and with sandwiches and salads like these, who can blame them? Calm then descends, and *Verde* gets back to being a superb boutique food shop where Harvey sources both staple and luxury with equal care. A regular customer might arrive, lucky thing, to do her weekly shop which Harvey has thought out for her in advance according to what delights he has in the cold store downstairs. This is food shopping as it should be.

---

imbibe / devour:
rose harissa
homemade marmalade
pierre marcolini chocolates
l'antica madia nettle pasta
capirete 20 year old sherry vinegar
moutarde verte a l'estragon
cassoulet au confit d'oie
great sandwiches to order

william curley

contemporary chocolatier, patissier and dessert bar

32 - 34 shepherd market, w1j 7qn. between white horse and curzon streets

jubilee / piccadilly / victoria : green park

020 7495 0302 www.williamcurley.co.uk

mon - wed 10a - 9.30p thu - sat 10a - 10p

opened in 2007. owners: william and suzue curley

$$: all major credit cards accepted

coffee / tea. treats. first come, first served

mayfair > **e44**

I died and went to heaven when I came to *William Curley*. I. Love. Chocolate. Oh, god, yes I do. Now I can come here and have the single most delicious chocolate experience of my sheltered life again and again. Thanks to William and Suzue, my new death row meal (a favourite game in our house) has the chocolate tarte here as pudding, no question. I was put on to this place by John at *Teasmith*, himself also a Scotsman married to a Japanese woman. Thank you, John. So what to call the beautiful, cross-cultural aesthetic at play here? McZen? No, that will never catch on. Answers on a postcard, please.

imbibe / devour:
spiced hot chocolate
aztec chilli infused hot chocolate
tarte au chocolat
chuao single estate ganache
handmade chocolates with:
  fresh mint
  szechuan pepper
  sea salted caramel

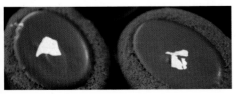

wright brothers

oyster and porter house

11 stoney street, se1 9ad. between winchester walk and park street
jubilee / northern : london bridge
020 7403 9554 www.wrightbros.eu.com
mon - fri noon - 10.30p hot food noon - 3p and 6 - 10.30p
sat 11a - 10.30p hot food 11a - 4p and 6 - 10.30p

opened in 2005. owners: robin hancock and ben wright chef: david burke
$$: all major credit cards accepted
brunch. lunch. dinner. full bar. reservations recommended

borough >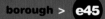

We all agreed that it feels like we've been coming here for years. I say 'we all' because as soon as I mentioned *Wright Brothers*, Hege had booked a table and invited another friend along. We feasted. I knew that the seafood was going to be super fresh because these guys supply many fine restaurants. What I hadn't anticipated was how brilliantly Chef David has worked out the menu. An example: beef and oyster pie comes with the oysters on the side. You crack a hole in the top of the pie and pour in the oysters. Oooh. He should be proud.

imbibe / devour:
pitfield 1850 london porter
champagne
rockefeller tapas oysters misted with pernod
wasabi tapas oysters
baked scallops with sauce vierge
fish soup with rouille
fish pie
beef & oyster pie

eat.shop.sleep and more

there are many great places to stay in london, but here are a few of my picks:

the zetter
st. john's square. 86-88 clerkenwell road
thezetter.com
standard double from £160

my hotel chelsea
35 ixworth place
myhotels.com
standard double from £140

hazlitt's and the rookery
hazlitt's: 6 frith street. soho square
the rookery: 12 peter's lane
hazlittshotel.com
standard double from £250

portobello hotel
22 stanley gardens
portobellohotel.com
standard double from £190

the firmdale hotels including my favorite:
covent garden hotel
10 monmouth street
firmdale.com
standard double from £350

k west hotel & spa
44 glenthorne road
k-west.co.uk
standard double from £130

beyond eating and shopping, here are some suggestions:

dennis severs house (dennissevershouse.co.uk) > this is a walk-through experience of an eighteenth century london house, complete with a narrative of the family through sounds and smells - indescribable and not to be missed.

sir john soane's museum (soane.org) > an eclectic house with a fantastic collection of art in the centre of town .

royal botanic gardens aka kew gardens (kew.org) > afterwards you can have tea at the nearby maids of honour tea rooms for an old-fashioned treat... i can't seem to get away from the eating thing.

horniman museum & gardens (horniman.ac.uk) > if you have children in town, this is a fabulous place full of odd insect and stuffed animal collections, an aquarium and lovely exhibitions plus a garden with animals.

hampstead heath (cityoflondon.gov.uk/corporation/living_environment/open_spaces/hampstead_heath. htm) > the most wonderful place with native woodland and fantastic views of the city. in the summer you can swim in the idyllic women's pond, the very cruisey male pond or parliament hill lido if you fancy. you can have lunch, or tea in kenwood house, or at café mozart on west end lane. just come here and get lost for a while.

westminster, waterloo + borough

eat

e5 > el vergel
e32 > shipps tearooms
e38 > the cinnamon club
e45 > wright brothers

shop

s35 > radio days

note: all maps face north

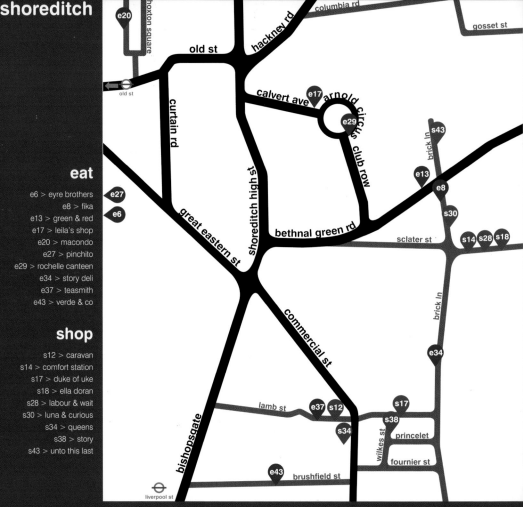

shoreditch

eat

e6 > eyre brothers
e8 > fika
e13 > green & red
e17 > leila's shop
e20 > macondo
e27 > pinchito
e29 > rochelle canteen
e34 > story deli
e37 > teasmith
e43 > verde & co

shop

s12 > caravan
s14 > comfort station
s17 > duke of uke
s18 > ella doran
s28 > labour & wait
s30 > luna & curious
s34 > queens
s38 > story
s43 > unto this last

note: all maps face north

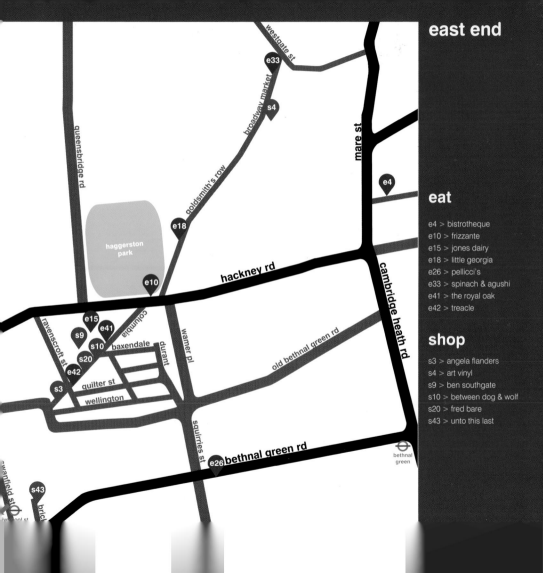

east end

eat

e4 > bistrotheque
e10 > frizzante
e15 > jones dairy
e18 > little georgia
e26 > pellicci's
e33 > spinach & agushi
e41 > the royal oak
e42 > treacle

shop

s3 > angela flanders
s4 > art vinyl
s9 > ben southgate
s10 > between dog & wolf
s20 > fred bare
s43 > unto this last

marylebone

eat

e14 > green valley
e16 > la fromagerie
e19 > locanda locatelli
e40 > the golden hind

shop

s2 > alfie's antiques market
s27 > joel & son

note: all maps face north

mayfair
+ st. james

eat

e44 > william curley

eat

s1 > albam
s5 > b store
s8 > bates
s15 > d. r. harris
s22 > geo f. trumper

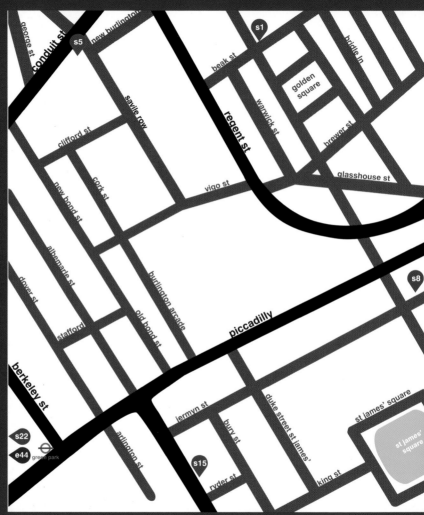

note: all maps face north

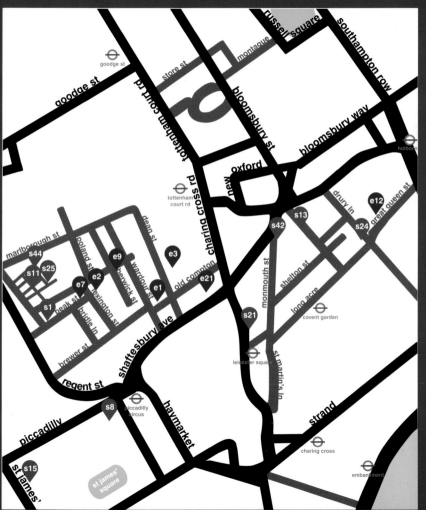

soho + covent garden

eat

e1 > algerian coffee stores
e2 > andrew edmunds
e3 > barrafina
e7 > fernandez & wells
e9 > flat white
e12 > great queen street
e21 > maison bertaux

shop

s1 > albam
s8 > bates
s11 > beyond the valley
s13 > coffee, cake & kink
s15 > d. r. harris
s21 > g smith & sons
s24 > happie loves it
s25 > hurwundeki
s42 > two see
s44 > victim

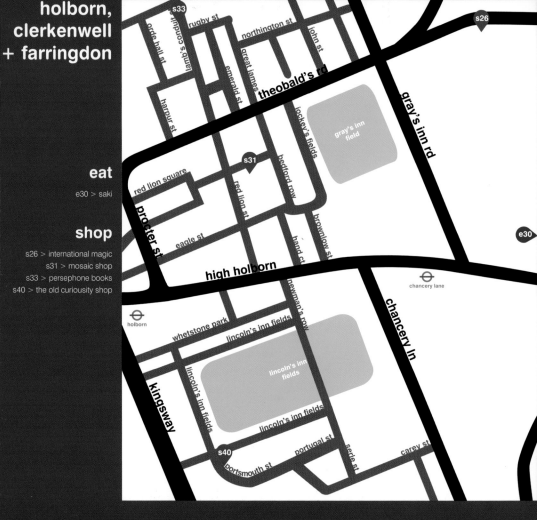

holborn, clerkenwell + farringdon

eat

e30 > saki

shop

s26 > international magic
s31 > mosaic shop
s33 > persephone books
s40 > the old curiousity shop

note: all maps face north

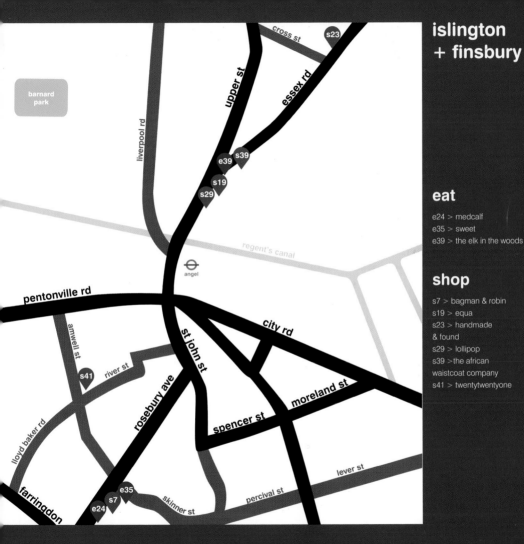

islington
+ finsbury

eat

e24 > medcalf
e35 > sweet
e39 > the elk in the woods

shop

s7 > bagman & robin
s19 > equa
s23 > handmade
& found
s29 > lollipop
s39 > the african
waistcoat company
s41 > twentytwentyone

note: all maps face north

albam

simple and modern men's classics
23 beak street, w1f 9rs. at upper john street
piccadilly / bakerloo : piccadilly circus
020 3157 7000 www.albamclothing.com
mon - sat 11a - 7p sun noon - 5p

opened in 2007. owners: james shaw and alastair rae
all major credit cards accepted
online shopping. custom orders

soho > **s01**

Autumn at Alb...
Fisherman's Cagoule
Bullitt Mac
Chunky Zip Cardigan
Grey Marl Sweatshirt
Classic White Shirt
Bengal Stripe Kennedy S
Egyptian Cotton T Shirt:
Straight Leg Jean
Black Boat Shoe
Leather Weave Belt
Weekend Travel Ba...

Albam is a special place. They make great men's clothes. Simple, stylish, well made. It's this type of shop, you know, where everything fits and looks super and you come out looking a little bit more like Steve McQueen. I am, it must be said, jealous. *Albam* is also run by people who care deeply about every detail. If you get James talking cloth, for example, you too will learn words like selvedge (the uncut edge of fabric). You'll also care about quality... ooh, yes, feel the quality. And everything here, bar the shirts, is made in England. Brilliant.

covet:
albam:
  "bullitt" mac
  classic white shirt
  lambswool scarf
  camel fisherman's cardigan
  chocolate brown suede belt
  leather overnight bag
  "rite in the rain" all-weather journal

105

alfie's antiques market

three floors of fun

13 - 25 church street, nw8 8dt. between ashbridge street and lisson grove
bakerloo : marylebone / edgware road
020 7723 6066 www.alfiesantiques.com
tue - sat 10a - 6p

opened in 1976. owner: bennie gray
mc. visa

marylebone > s02

Oh, please, Kaie, (publisher and *eat.shop* goddess) please, can *Alfie's* be in? I know that three floors of collectable lighting, design classics and couture vintage on a road of twenty independent antique furniture shops is kind of cheating for one entry in this book but… I'm up to my limit on shops and would have trouble choosing just one place from in here. There's *Decoratum* for their exquisite 20th century collectable furniture, but what about *Heaven of Gowns* for fashion or *Vincenzo Caffarella* for lighting? I spent a whole rainy afternoon wandering these floors and I loved it.

covet:
'30s architect-designed furniture (bentply)
'70s danish light (lorna lee leslie)
scapinelli coffee table (decoratum)
'60s mazzega chandeliers (vincenzo caffarella)
vintage couture (heaven of gowns)
eero aarnio bubble chair (francesca martire)

angela flanders

perfumer

96 columbia road, e2 7qb. between ravenscroft and gossett streets
central : bethnal green <or> northern : old street <or>
central / circle / hammersmith & city / metropolitan : liverpool street
020 7739 7555 www.angelaflanders_perfumier.com
sun 9a - 2.30p or by appointment

opened in 1985. owner: angela flanders
all major credit cards accepted
gift baskets to order. custom orders. gift vouchers

columbia road > **s03**

I've a very few scents that I stick with, but I'm going to add an *Angela Flanders* creation to my list. I haven't yet plumped for which one, but there are a couple of strong contenders. They smell ni-i-ice. Angela laughingly describes this shop as her fourth attempt at retirement. Yes, she did a few other interesting things before she became a perfumer, and all that life experience adds to the atmosphere here. It's a scent heaven, with smells for both sexes and for around the home. So while you're at the Sunday flower market, dive in here for olfactory fun and frolics.

covet:
angela flanders:
   jasmine single flower note fragrance
   bouquet d'amour special-edition perfume
   poudrée perfume
   bois de seville scented candle
   mr. severs scented candle
   coromandel ambiance room spray
   orange flowers linen perfume

art vinyl

art and music meet in vinyl frame shop

13 broadway market, e8 4ph. corner of jackman street. central : bethnal green
020 7241 4129 www.artvinyl.com
thu - sun 11a - 6p

opened in 2005. owner: andrew heeps
mc. visa
online shopping. gallery

broadway market > s04

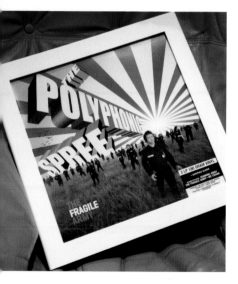

Sometimes a one-trick pony has such a good trick that you have to stand back and applaud. Or put it in your book, in my case. *Art Vinyl* sells frames that put your favourite album artwork onto your wall. The frames also tilt open, allowing easy access, making them a clever storage system. And don't forget the vinyl. They sell it here, both new and old. While shopping here on Saturdays, watch Broadway Market come alive with interesting clothes designers, great food (see *Spinach & Agushi*) and a soundtrack courtesy of Andrew and his invited dj's.

covet:
play & display:
  matt black frames
  ice white frames
  triple pack
  gift pack (including an album)
new & vintage vinyl, 12"s & lps:
  st. germain: tourist
  soul of man: mylowdowndirty / foxy moron

b store

I knew that *B Store* was going to be great even before I saw it. I lost count of how many people had raved about it, many of them other boutique owners. So, I came. Yes, I can now say with authority, *B Store* is all it's cracked up to be. It rocks. If you love fashion and talented young designers, this place is a mecca, with the work of thirty designers in one supremely elegant space. Matthew and Kirk even design their own *B* line. There's so much fashion talent in here it throbs. And I mean that in a good way.

covet:
carola euler
damir doma
diana brinks
hartmann nordenholz
michelle lowe-holder
siv stoldar
ute ploier
stephan schneider

b tailoring

visiting bespoke tailor
wherever you are in london, peter will be
07957 745 163 www.btailoring.co.uk
mon - fri 9a - 6p

opened in 1997. owner: peter bramley
mc. visa
custom orders / design

where you are > **s06**

Peter Bramley is a visiting tailor, meaning, he comes to you. Yes, that's right. Peter, with twenty years experience, comes to you. Nice, huh? The process works like this: at first meeting, Peter measures and makes decisions with you on cloth, shape and style. Then the suit is made in Yorkshire, the home of British wool and tailoring. About a month later you have a forward fitting, where Peter tweaks, pins and chalks. Another month, and there's a final fitting. Presto, you have a bespoke suit, and for a fraction of the cost of Savile Row. You will sing "I know it's going to fit" like Ian Dury, you lucky man.

covet:
men's tailored clothing in worsted, merino, cashmere or tweed wool, linen or cotton:
   suits
   trousers
   jackets
   shooting outfits
   shirts

bagman and robin

fashion bags and accesories
47 exmouth market, ec1r 4ql. between farringdon road and skinner street
northern : angel <or> circle / hammersmith & city / metropolitan : farringdon
020 7561 9865 www.bagmanandrobin.com
mon - sat 11a - 6p

opened in 2006. owners: marco araldi and keng wai lee
all major credit cards accepted
custom orders

farringdon > s07

I have a bag thing, so *Bagman and Robin* is right up my alley. Marco and Lee take vintage Japanese and Liberty fabrics and make wonderful bags out of them. My partner Simon saw the light in my eyes when I was here with him and bought me a bangle bag for Christmas. Now I'm just waiting for a party so I can hang my oh-so-clever bag on my arm from its bangle while I nibble and sip with both hands free. It's January so I may have to wait a while. "Enjoy Your Bag" is the *Bagman and Robin* motto and let's face it, who can quibble with that?

covet:
pochette evening bags
kika day shoulder / shopper bags
piu piu bangle bags
bag door stops
handmade belts
mo hand moulded leather manbags
handmade felt pieces

bates

gentlemen's hatters

21a jermyn street, sw1y 6hp. between regent and babmaes streets
bakerloo / picadilly : picadilly circus
020 7734 2722 www.bates-hats.co.uk
mon - fri 9a - 5p sat 9.30a - 1p sun 2 - 4p

opened in 1902. owner: tim boucher
all major credit cards accepted
online shopping

st. james' > s08

As a teenager, I was given a wide-brimmed, bottle green fedora from *Bates* by my mother. It really suited me. I loved it beyond all measure. Then, in Paris, I left it in a phone box, and when I went back, it was gone. I was so gutted that I couldn't bring myself to replace it. It just didn't seem right. Today, when I went to *Bates* to take these pictures, I thought, yes, the pain has gone. But now I'm torn between a baker boy or that fedora. So I'm thinking on it. *Bates* is a gentleman's hatter par excellence. But they don't mind serving us ladies, too. Which is very good news indeed, for all.

covet:
bates hats:
  fedora
  baker boys & gatsbys
  deerstalkers
  flat caps
  trilbys
panama hats
top hats

ben southgate

furniture dealer and restorer

4 the courtyard. ezra street, e2 7rh. courtyard entrance off columbia road
northern : old street <or> central : bethnal green <or>
central / circle / hammersmith & city / metropolitan : liverpool street
07905 960792 www.bsouthgate.co.uk
sun 9a - 2.30p

opened in 2003. owner: ben southgate
mc. visa

columbia road > s09

Ben Southgate specialises in oak furniture. He spends his week scouring furniture sales and restoring the pieces in his workshop. Then on Sundays, Ben brings them here to sell. Along the way, of course, he finds other pleasing things besides oak furniture. The "popular puzzle" of the war years and leather suitcases catch his eye. As for Columbia Road Sunday flower market, once a week it erupts, full of life and colour. The shops around it only open for a few hours of Sunday, too, and are, like butterflies, English asparagus, or Seville oranges—especially to be treasured.

covet:
oak table & chairs
german medical cabinet
table football
aluminium coat rack
bakelite-lidded kitchen storage jars
numbered hooks
leather suitcases
bakelite filing trays

between dog & wolf

elegant artisan-made gardenalia

130 columbia road, e2 7rg. between ezra and ravenscroft streets
northern : old street <or> central : bethnal green <or>
central / circle / hammersmith & city / metropolitan : liverpool street
07961 415460 www.betweendogandwolf.com
sun 9.30a - 2.30p

opened in 2006. owner: charlotte van cuylenburg
all major credit cards accepted
tools can be specialised to order or engraved

columbia road > s10

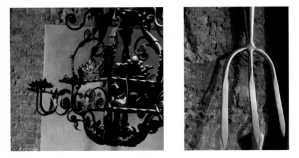

Charlotte has exquisite taste. That can be the only explanation as to why *Between Dog & Wolf* is such a heavenly place to come to. I mean, gardening tools, terracotta pots, books, wine, lotions and potions… it sounds so busy, it can't work, can it? Well, it can and does, and I keep coming back. Everything here is the finest, most handmade, most beautiful, just… the most. This place, along with the whole of Columbia Road, is only open when the flower market is: on Sundays, and Charlotte has a full-time job the rest of the week. So you know that this is a true labour of love.

covet:
santa maria novella weekend iris soap
sneeboer hand-forged gardening tools
kuyen biodynamic wine from chile
hand thrown whichford terracotta pots
moist potpourri aged in wax-sealed urns
sali di bagno fragranced with pomegranate
"dear friend and gardener"
  by christopher lloyd & beth chatto

123

beyond the valley

young designers doing it for themselves
2 newburgh street, w1f 7rd. between ganton street and foubert's place
central / victoria : oxford circus
020 7437 7338 www.beyondthevalley.com
mon - sat 11.30a - 7.30p sun 12.30 - 6p

opened in 2005. owners: kate harwood, jo jackson and kristjana s. williams
all major credit cards accepted
online shopping. registries. gallery

soho > s11

Shop, gallery, hothouse, stepping stone, creative community and commercially successful in Soho. You've got to hand it to these three young design grads. I want to hand it to them... my credit card, that is. I'm trying really, really hard not to break my don't-shop-on-the-job rule and at *Beyond the Valley* it's impossible. Thank god that I cycled into town today. I console myself with the thought that no one wants a thoughtful, witty present that's been squashed. So I will have to come back. Soon. Tomorrow.

covet:
beyond the valley:
  womenswear, menswear & funky mirrors
yuko yoshitake
jojo & malou
donna wilson knitted imagined creatures
miss bibi jewelery
marcello toshi shoes
wattson electricity sensor by diy kyoto

125

caravan

style for sale

11 lamb street, e1 6ea. between commercial and steward streets
central / circle / metropolitan / hammersmith & city : liverpool street
020 7247 6467 www.caravanstyle.com
tue - fri 11a - 6p sat 1 - 5p sun 11a - 5p

opened in 2005. owner: emily chambers
all major credit cards accepted
online shopping. registries. custom orders

spitalfields > **s12**

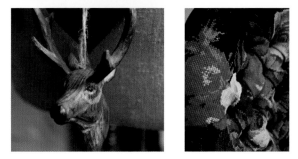

I think *Caravan* should be available by prescription to cure the grey day blues. Yes, you guessed it, it's a grey day as I type this, but looking back over my pictures of *Caravan* has brought the sun into the room. Emily's magpie stylist's eye gathers together a visual feast. From big things like furniture down to the teeniest knitted dogs, every single treasure is delicious. The titles of her own books give you clues as to her aesthetic: "Flea Market Style" and "Contemporary Country." She's stunningly stylish and sickeningly prolific and I want to be her friend. And to live in her shop. Please?

covet:
vintage floral fabric-covered mannequins
vintage floral fabric skirts, bags & lampshades
french industrial style lamps
hand-blown glass bauble droplets
silver clogs
recycled tyre bins & plant pots
magnetic insects
reflective winged bicycle clips

coffee, cake & kink

kinky café, shop and gallery

61 endell street, wc2h 9aj. between high holborn and shorts gardens
piccadilly : covent garden <or> central : tottenham court road
020 7419 2996 www.coffeecakeandkink.com
sun - thu 11a - 8p fri - sat 11a - 11p

opened in 2003. owner: alan cassidy
all major credit cards accepted
online shopping. gallery

covent garden > **s13**

Why, I hear you ask, is a place that begins with the words coffee and cake in the shop side? Well, as a café, this place is a curiosity, but as a purveyor of things to do with sex, it's unique. It's bright and friendly, and it calmly celebrates open-minded, pan-sexual, pan-gender, joyful kinkiness and exuberant sexuality. So while you have a freshly ground cafetière of coffee, you can check out the range of carefully chosen items for both sexes and educate yourself on anything from burlesque to the fetish scene. Or just eat chocolate cake and read the paper. They don't mind how you do it.

covet:
marcus gray figurines
i rub my duckie vibrating waterproof rubber duck
fun factory smartballs
ohmibod (vibrates to the music on your ipod)
goldfrau ceramic dildos
ostrich feather ticklers
books & manuals on topics from
  burlesque to spanking

comfort station

witty, romantic jewelery and accessories

22 cheshire street, e2 6eh. between brick lane and chilton street
central / circle / hammersmith & city / metropolitan : liverpool street
020 7033 9099 www.comfortstation.co.uk
tue - sun 11a - 6p

opened in 2004. owner: amy anderson
all major credit cards accepted
order by email. custom orders

brick lane > **s14**

I was at *Comfort Station* just before Christmas. While I was there, not one but two men came in, separately, and said that the last piece of Amy's jewelery they had bought for their loved ones had gone down so well that they were back for more. Then they browsed, bought, and left happy. Thumbs up to them. I now leave *Comfort Station* business cards around all over the house for Simon to notice but so far, no luck. I'll give him until after Valentine's Day. But that's it. If he doesn't deliver, I'm going to go in and buy myself one of the absurdly talented Amy's unique creations.

covet:
comfort station:
  book pendant with poem inside
  heart clock pendant
  "cover me in dust" necklace
  tempus fugit bracelet
  cuckoo-clock necklace
  clambag handbag
  bone china mugs

d.r. harris & co. ltd

chemists and perfumers

29 st. james's street, sw1a 1hb. between jermyn and ryder streets
jubilee / piccadilly / victoria : green park
020 7930 3915 www.drharris.co.uk
mon - fri 8.30a - 6p sat 9.30a - 5p

opened in 1790. owner: d. r. harris
all major credit cards accepted
online shopping

st. james' > s15

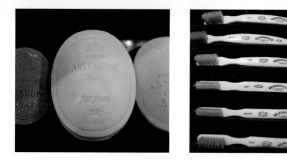

My London pre-Christmas ritual always includes a visit to *D.R. Harris*. It's the perfect place for all those hard-to-buy-for people. Like family. It's a dispensing pharmacy, too, as well as a lotions and potions emporium, so you can get all your bathroom cabinet staples here and your prescription drugs, too. The highlights for me, though, are the luxurious things: triple-milled soap, bone-handled toothbrushes, sandalwood aftershave and his and hers bath essences. The one thing I've never given as a gift is the *Harris* pick-me-up. Well, you wouldn't, would you? But I bet it works.

covet:
almond oil soaps
pure bristle body brush
sandalwood aftershave
shaving soaps & creams
combs made from horn
harris pick-me-up
fern bath oil
verbena bath essence

divette

boudoir boutique for women

unit 6: portobello green, 218 portobello road, w10 5tz
under the westway between cambridge gardens and lancaster road
hammersmith & city : ladbroke grove <or> central / circle / district : notting hill gate
020 8969 4653 www.divette.co.uk
tue - sat 10.30a - 5.30p

opened in 2004. owner: ivette laviola
all major credit cards accepted
online shopping

portobello > 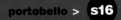 **s16**

Across the road from the *Makan Café* is Portobello Green and here be treasures, as the pirates say. My son Jonjo is five, so I think this way. Enjoy your wander through this little arcade with its twenty designers, and make sure to stop in at *Divette* to check out Ivette's range of undies and bedroom-wear. Everything is wonderfully feminine and sexy without looking like it's trying too hard. I want to look effortlessly gorgeous, please. Ah, good, I've just found my New Year's resolution. And it's only the 24th of January, so just in time.

covet:
divette:
   organic silk undies & bedroomwear
   frilly knickers
lou lingerie
freya large-cup bras
eberjey lingerie
sensualle brazilian thongs
bacirubati lingerie

duke of uke

ukulele and banjo emporium

22 hanbury street, e1 6qr. between wilkes street and brick lane
central / circle / hammersmith & city / metropolitan : liverpool street
020 7247 7924 www.dukeofuke.co.uk
tue - sun noon - 7p

opened in 2006. owner: matthew reynolds
mc. visa
online shopping. classes. custom orders

spitalfields > **s17**

In Britain, the saying "It does exactly what it says on the tin" has become currency, thanks to a brain-worm television ad for, I think, wood sealant. Anyway, you see where I'm going here… in the *Duke of Uke* you will, of course, find all things ukulele. Plus quite a bit more. There's a recording studio downstairs, for instance. Plus Matthew runs club and party nights with cabaret and art performances as well as live music. It shouldn't surprise me that *Duke of Uke* is so cool. I'm having to rethink my whole take on the uke. Bye-bye George Formby (type his name in You Tube) and his window cleaning.

covet:
mele ukelele
g string uke
banjos
banjoleles
mxr pedals
danelectro
range of guitars
books of dots & chords

137

ella doran

luscious homeware
46 cheshire street, e2 6eh. at chilton
district / hammersmith & city : aldgate east <or>
circle / central / hammersmith & city / metropolitan : liverpool street
020 7613 0782 www.elladoran.co.uk
sat noon - 5p sun 11a - 5p tue - fri or by appointment

opened in 2005. owner: ella doran
all major credit cards accepted
online shopping. custom orders / design

brick lane > **s18**

I saw an interview once with Chet Baker, and his advice was: work out what it is you like to do, become the best there is at it and you'll be fine. It worked for Chet and it works for *Ella Doran* too. She's an unfeasibly talented designer, originally of textiles, who can fill your home with her photographic images printed onto everything from placemats to blinds. So this shop is like a sunny day in a field of flowers, full of colour and beauty. They sell things they like by other people too, so you'll find all manner of loveliness sourced from all over the place.

covet:
ella doran:
  mugs
  blinds
  trays
  bookmarks
  placemats
genevieve berrin raku
roundabout memory game

equa

fair trade and organic fashion
28 camden passage, n1 8ed. between duncan street and charlton place
northern : angel
020 7359 0955 www.equaclothing.com
mon 11a - 6p tue 10.30a - 6p wed - fri 10.30a - 6.30p
sat 10a - 6.30p sun noon - 5p

opened in 2005. owner: penelope cook
all major credit cards accepted
online shopping

islington > **s19**

While researching this book, I wandered into a great ethical fashion fair. The labels that I loved there noted *Equa* as their London stockist, so I followed the lead. Ladies, here is our chance to look good and feel good too—with wit, to boot. Example: Greenknickers make (surprise!) knickers in organic, fair-trade cotton, naturally. On one pair, a globe design on the front warms as you wear them, and the continents disappear. Nice touch. Penelope has a great buyer's eye. Several shoppers in here had no idea that the clothes were worthy; they just knew they looked good. Even better.

covet:
people tree
annie greenabelle
terraplana offcut leather shoes
enamore lingerie
alchem1st dresses & leather bags
loomstate denim
edun denim & dresses
po-zu slippers

fred bare

hip hat shop

118 columbia road, e2 7rg. between barnet grove and ravenscroft street
northern : old street <or> central : bethnal green <or>
central / circle / hammersmith & city / metropolitan : liverpool street
020 7729 6962 www.fredbare.co.uk
sun 9a - 2.30p

opened in 1990. owner: anita evagora
all major credit cards accepted
online shopping

columbia road > 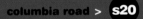 **s20**

You might have guessed that I am fond of a titfer (titfer=tit for tat=hat). I think it all stems from the time I was told, aged thirteen, that I would have to have a riding hat made for me as they did not do hats big enough, even in the men's department. Now this is not what a teenage girl needs to hear. It's ok, I'm over it now. But, ever since, I have reveled in any headgear that fits. So I love *Fred Bare*, which is another Columbia Road shop that really rewards getting up on a Sunday morning. The hats here have "it" in spades. Some of them even fit me.

covet:
fred bare wool, straw, felt and cotton:
  hats
  beanies
  cloches
  caps
  berets
  sun hats

g. smith & sons

tobacconists, snuff blenders and cigar importers
74 charing cross road, wc2h 0bg. between lichfield and great newport streets
northern / piccadilly : leicester square
020 7836 7422
mon - fri 9a - 6p sat 9.30a - 5.30p

opened in 1869. owner: jeremy cole
all major credit cards accepted

between soho and covent garden > s21

"It's tobacco. It's one of the healthiest things for your body. Now go ahead." Ah, bollocks... no, of course, that's in a movie (*Sleeper*). *G. Smith & Sons* was the first shop on Charing Cross road, built as a tobacconist, in the days when smoking was all the rage. Now smokers are social pariahs. But here is a world where there is nothing to hide. Many flavours of snuff beckon the brave or those challenged by the long-haul flight. The humidor is a whole room, so if cigars are your thing, or if you want to make a cigar lover very happy, step inside.

covet:
cuban cigars
classic pipes
sheffield-made clay pipes
the famous george iv snuff blend (blended here)
rosewood snuff boxes
leather tobacco pouches
american spirit tobacco & cigarettes
vanilla snuff

geo. f. trumper

traditional gentlemen's barber

9 curzon street, w1j 5hq. between clarges and queen street
jubilee / piccadilly / victoria : green park
020 7499 1850 www.trumpers.com
mon - fri 9a - 5.30p sat 9a - 1p

opened in 1875. owner: paulette bersch
all major credit cards accepted
online shopping. mail order. open razor shaving school

Gentlemen metrosexuals have been coming to *Trumper* for over a hundred years so, guys, go ahead and treat yourselves. But, hey, I'm female, what do I know? Well, the paraphernalia is gorgeous, for starters, and as I was taking photos, men from eighteen to eighty were coming and going in an atmosphere of efficient service and restrained pleasure. I gave Simon a gift voucher for a wet shave with hot towels and a haircut at *Trumper* for Christmas. He went last week. He looks good. See, I do know something.

covet:
wet shave & hot towels
haircut & shampoo
beard trim
mini facial
bristle hairbrushes
trumper range of colognes & aftershaves
badger brush shaving sets
open razors & hanging strops

handmade & found

stylish and unusual women's fashion
109 essex road, n1 2sl. beside the corner of cross street
northern : angel <or> victoria / overground : highbury & islington
020 7359 3898 www.handmadeandfound.co.uk
tue - sat 10.30a - 6p

opened in 1998. owners: anthony wilson and ruth llewllyn
mc. visa
occasional custom orders

islington > **s23**

Handmade & Found: handmade pieces emerge from the workshop at the back, courtesy of Ruth. Anthony sources the found collection as well as stocks pieces by young and unsung Japanese and Korean designers. It's really two shops in one, but since Anthony's and Ruth's tastes complement each other beautifully, it works for me. While I was last in here, a wonderfully diverse regular clientele came in, checking out what was new. There was a boyfriend bringing in his girlfriend to show her a piece. Isn't it usually the other way around? I saw this as a great sign.

covet:
found silk shirt dress with box-pleated neckline
handmade floral shirts
handmade skirts in matching colours
dree
pgpc
tsumori chisato
quirky jewelery

happie loves it

carefree print dresses and tops
37 drury lane, wc2b 5rr. at great queen street
central / piccadilly : holborn <or> piccadilly : covent garden
020 7379 5455 www.happielovesit.com
mon - wed 10.30a - 7.30p thu - fri 10.30a - 8p sat 10a - 7p sun noon - 5p

opened in 2007. owners: seung han and happie
mc. visa

covent garden > 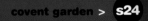 **s24**

A couple of years ago I bought a great floral-print shirt dress in the small labels section of Topshop by *Happie Loves It*. I looked them up online, but there was nothing. Then today, after a restaurant shoot, I spied this shop and got excited. Very excited indeed. The designers are Korean and live in London, and their prints are absolute heaven. When I entered the boutique, I saw that they even had a different colour-way of my now very worn favourite dress. Hallelujah. And so I present to you *Happie Loves It*. I do, too.

covet:
metallicized tweed coat
ice-cream appliqué dress with hood
floral shirt dresses
print dresses
gossamer floral dresses
wide elasticated black belt
tights & leg warmers in one

hurwundeki

modern, affordable clothes for men and women
34 marshall street, w1f 7eu. between ganton street and foubert's place
bakerloo / central / victoria : oxford circus
020 7734 1050 www.hurwundeki.com (see website for second location)
mon - sat 11a - 7p sun noon - 5p

opened in 2007. owner: ki lee
mc. visa

soho > **s25**

Kaie and I fell upon this Soho outpost of *Hurwundeki* (the original is in Spitalfields) on its opening day. We both lit up as soon as we walked in here with its bare brick walls and light pouring in. Upstairs is menswear, downstairs womenswear plus a small vintage room. For me, the real stars are *Hurwundeki's* own label of afford-able, structured pieces. Today I'm wearing the asym-metrical hooded grey wool sweater I bought on that first day, just before I imposed my no-buying-on-the-job rule. It's been my winter stalwart. Kaie bought a dress. (Kaie note: I love and live in this dress.) Say no more.

covet:
hurwundeki:
  asymmetrical hooded grey wool jumper (!)
  herringbone coat with tie belt
  grey dress with pleated front
  black short sleeved-dress with pockets
  felt cloche hat
  rubber ankle boots
  white crackleglaze effect boots

153

international magic

cool magic shop

89 clerkenwell road, ec1r 5bx. between leather lane and gray's inn road
circle / hammersmith & city / metropolitan / thameslink : farringdon
020 7405 7324 www.internationalmagic.com
mon - fri 11.30a - 6p sat 11.30a - 4p

opened in 1962. owner: martin macmillan
all major credit cards accepted
online shopping. classes

clerkenwell > **s26**

I know someone who has travelled around rural India. His most useful travel tip? Not pharmaceuticals for every emergency, or *The Ultimate Backpackers Guide*. In his pocket he carried the magic vanishing handkerchief trick, which was his calling card in every tiny village where no one spoke English. Genius. At *International Magic* you can learn and buy great illusions and, while you may not reach, say, Ricky Jay's level of expertise, you too can stun your friends with your newfound prowess. Just don't bring any funny decks to the poker table. Not with me, anyway.

covet:
cups & balls
magic vanishing handkerchief
supernatural coin trick
range of instructional / performance dvds
magic wand
wigs & moustaches
corinda's classic book on mentalism

joel & son

fantastic fabric shop

75 - 83 church street, nw8 8eu. between penfold street and lisson grove
bakerloo : edgware road / marylebone
020 7724 6895 www.joelandsonfabrics.com
mon - sat 9a - 5p

opened in 1981. owner: joel bull
all major credit cards accepted

marylebone > **s27**

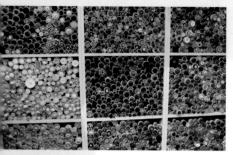

Beehive. Ants nest. I'm trying to think of a good way to describe *Joel & Son* that doesn't involve insects. The place is one vast space, floor to ceiling rolls of fabric, with people scurrying about serving customers in subdued tones. Occasionally a cry goes up: "Mr. J, Mr. J," and Joel hurries over to give his expertise. He is lovely. As he showed me around, and I wished I could sew, Mr. J replied, quick as a flash, "There are evening classes, young lady. You can learn." I felt empowered. I thought, yes, I can learn. I'll try, Mr. J, I'll try.

covet:
lora piana cashmere
silks by valentino
laces from france & italy
metallic chantilly lace
italian silk shantung
cotton shirt fabrics
giupurre lace
italian pure wool

labour and wait

elegant and timeless homeware

18 cheshire street, e2 6eh. between poland and ramillies streets
bakerloo / central / victoria : oxford circus
020 7729 6253 www.labourandwait.co.uk
fri by appointment sat 1 - 5p sun 10a - 5p

opened in 2000. owners: simon watkins and rachel wythe-moran
mc. visa
online shopping

brick lane > s28

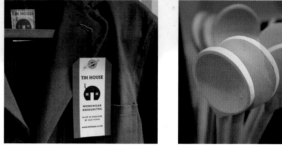

My desert island shop? *Labour and Wait*, no question. Here you will find special things that will always work and become invaluable to your daily existence. Here they source the places where these treasures are still made, and then they bring them to you. The perfect zester? The doormat that cleans my shoes? The ostrich feather duster so glamourous that it makes me dust? All here. Plus so much more. Form and function meet in a timeless oasis of calm that provides the perfect antidote to the bustle of Brick Lane. Life on a desert island? With *Labour and Wait*, no problem.

covet:
ostrich feather duster
rope doorstop
twine on oak stand
horn egg spoon
the perfect outside dooormat
fisherman's smock from great yarmouth, norfollk
guernsey sweaters
knitted tea cosy

lollipop

lovely shoe shop

114 islington high street, n1 8eg. between charlton place and duncan street
northern : angel
020 7226 4005 www.lollipoplondon.com
mon - wed 11a - 6p thu - sat 11a - 7p sun 2 - 5p

opened in 2005. owner: laura allnatt
all major credit cards accepted
online shopping

islington > **s29**

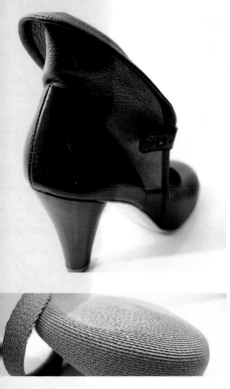

I went in search of *Intercol*, an emporium of playing cards, maps, coins and oddities but discovered that it has gone virtual and in its place is this lovely shoe shop filled with fabulous foot fashion. I mourn when one of my favourite quirky shops croaks, but when something as pleasing as this takes its place, it's like seeing the bulbs coming up after a long winter. Renewal, rebirth (cue the orchestral crescendo), tears well in the eyes, and I take my boots off in readiness to start trying things on. To keep things sweet, they have hats and bags, too. Yes, you see, *Lollipop* knows.

covet:
shoes:
  chie mihara
  avril gau
  jackson twins
  esska
  lollipop brand coming soon!
muhlbauer hats
heba nouman bags

luna & curious

eclectic design collective

198 brick lane, e1 6sa. corner of bacon street
circle / central / hammersmith & city / metropolitan : liverpool street <or>
district / hammersmith & city : aldgate east
020 7033 4411 www.lunaandcurious.com
thu - sun noon - 6p

opened in 2006. owners: carolyn corben, susie coulthard, polly george
jon harrison, natasha lawes and rheanna lingham
custom orders. gallery.   mc. visa

brick lane > s30

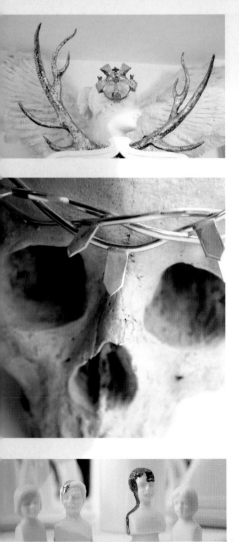

A cooperative of six designers plus friends. Sounds potentially interesting, you think? Well, that description is like calling Prince a short guy who plays the guitar. In terms of preparing you for the wonder and delight you will experience here, it doesn't come close. *Luna & Curious* is like walking through the back of the wardrobe into Narnia. This cooperative of emerging design talent is constantly evolving, and they have guest designers (the friends bit) who showcase here too. For me, it's quintessentially London. I love *Luna & Curious*—can you tell?

covet:
dresses made from vintage patterns in
    metallic paper
feathering service for shoes & bags
resin skulls
vintage shades
ceramic toast rack
jane haworth birds
locket necklace

mosaic shop

yep, it's a mosaic shop

1a princeton street, w1cr 4ax. between red lion street and bedford row
central / piccadilly : holborn
020 7831 0889 www.mosaicworkshop.com
wed - fri 10a - 5.30p

opened in 1999. owner: tessa hunkin
mc. visa
online shopping. classes. custom orders / design

holborn > s31

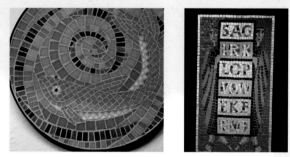

From the outside, the *Mosaic Shop* looks like a fantasy sweet shop, filled with jars of colour. Inside, it's a paradise of potential activity. There are complete mosaics for sale here, but you'll want to leave with a project, of which there are many. They'll teach you how to do it at classes or send you away with a kit complete with instructions. I once went to the Bardo Museum in Tunis where there are astounding room-sized Roman mosaics of Neptune riding sea monsters. I think I'll start with just one fish though, how about you?

covet:
mosaic kits
glass & ceramic tesserae
materials & tools
books on mosaic
finished mosaic wall pieces & sculptures
tessa's layered light boxes
handmade illuminated books

165

olive loves alfie

inspired children's clothing shop

84 stoke newington church street, n16 0ap. between bouverie and fleetwood roads
bus 73 from angel / oxford street <or> bus 476 from euston
020 7241 4212 www.olivelovesalfie.co.uk
mon - wed 9.30a - 5.30p thu 9.30a - 6.30p fri 9.30a - 5.30p sat 10a - 6p sun
noon - 5p

opened in 2007. owner: ashlyn gibson
all major credit cards accepted
online shopping

stoke newington > s32

Sooner or later in London, you outgrow the tube and take to the buses. One area only reached by bus is Stoke Newington Church Street, where there's plenty to explore. Take for example the cool kid's shop, *Olive Loves Alfie*. Ashlyn has got an amazing eye for a print. Where can grown-ups get prints like these? London is full of villages but few are lucky enough to have an Ashlyn blazing the style trail. Other villages to explore: Victoria Park Village, Northcote Road in Clapham or Lordship Lane in east Dulwich. But make *Olive Loves Alfie* your first bus mission and you'll be happy.

covet:
dandy star
rockabye baby
plastisock
katvig
authentic vintage clothing
djeco games & toys
gloverall duffle coats
lucky wang

persephone books

publisher of forgotten classics

59 lamb's conduit street, wc1n 3nb. between great ormond street and theobald's road

central / piccadilly : holborn

020 7242 9292 www.persephonebooks.co.uk

mon - fri 10a - 6p sat noon - 5p

opened in 1999. owner: nicola beauman

all major credit cards accepted

online shopping. mail order

bloomsbury > **s33**

When the pace of 21st century London gets to be too much, beat a path here and have a calm, leisurely browse. *Persephone Books* publishes neglected fiction and non-fiction, mainly by women, and they do it with élan. Each book is a thing of beauty, both on the outside and within. Bibliophiles, come. Design junkies, come. The bluestocking revolution begins here. There's nowhere else like it. Foodies, come too. The cookbooks are exquisite pieces of social and gastronomic history. Plus it's in on one of London's most charming streets. A haven.

covet:
someone at a distance by dorothy whipple
they can't ration these by vicomte de mauduit
saplings by noel streatfield
william - an englishman by cicely hamilton
good things in england by florence white
kitchen essays by agnes jekyll
how to run your home without help
  by kay smallshaw

169

queens

camp, kitsch décor fun

shop 111b, e1 6bg. off commercial in old spitalfields market
between lamb and brushfield streets
central / circle / metropolitan / hammersmith & city : liverpool street
020 7426 0017
tue - fri 11a - 6p sat noon - 5p sun 10a - 6p

opened in 1999. owners: gary ash and darren mckay
all major credit cards accepted

spitalfields > **s34**

Feeling a bit jaded? Lost your childish delight? Seen it all? I don't think so. Time to get on down to *Queens*, where it's always fairyland. My Christmas tree would look naked and wrong without its fairy bear from here. Does my son think that fish really do kiss? I must ask him. Sometimes among my friends, shops acquire new names: for example, there's "The Umbrella Shop" (*James Smith & Sons*) and, of course, "The Fairy Shop" which is another name for *Queens*. Now, say with me: "I do believe in fairies. I do. I do." Oh, come on, embrace the camp side. Feel the force.

covet:
ornaments:
  fairy teddy bear
  kissing fish
  supersonic space monkey
  elvis bear
  jellycat knitted robots
  merbaby in a bubble
dragonfly on wire

radio days

'20s - '70s clothing, collectables and memorabilia
87 lower marsh, se1 7ab. between johanna street and baylis road
bakerloo / jubilee / northern : waterloo
020 7928 0800 www.radiodaysvintage.co.uk
mon - sat 10a - 6p or by appointment

opened in 1993. owners: chrissie layzell and leroy william
mc. visa

waterloo > **s35**

Years ago, I stumbled upon *Radio Days* while I was rehearsing a play round the corner. I was hooked, and lunchbreaks became browse times as I delved deep. Happily they've rethought the layout since then, and now you can scan rather than rummage. Sometimes I need a break to think about what I've seen and whether or not I will use that cocktail set I found in which case I'll head for *Inshoku* for sushi or *Scooterworks for* coffee further along Lower Marsh. After I'm suitably revived, I'll return for the kill.

covet:
'40s sunglasses
'50s phones
vintage sheet music
'40s dresses
sequined tops
deco cufflinks
bakelite radios
vivien of holloway dresses

173

rellik

vintage couture for women
8 golborne road, w10 5nw. corner of hazlewood crescent
hammersmith & city : westbourne park
020 8962 0089 www.relliklondon.co.uk
tue - sat 10a - 6p

opened in 1999. owners: steben philip, clare stansfield and fiona stuart
all major credit cards accepted

portobello > **s36**

My Mother was a model—until Twiggy blew it for the curvaceous blonde with a big bust. My early memories involve make-up, Mum's big shoes and my gold and black child-size Biba dress. Glamour and style. *Rellik* has the feel of those memories in spades and is the most fabulous vintage shop ever. I watched a woman try on a little black dress that looked so fantastic on her that we all gasped. That's the *Rellik* moment, the one you hope for each time you come through the doors. If ever you needed proof that couture clothes are better than high street, it is here, where the quality shines through decades later.

covet:
vintage:
  vivienne westwood
  malcom mclaren
  body map
  ossie clark
  biba
  john galliano
  alaia

175

scarlet & violet

elegant, eccentric wabi-sabi florists

76 chamberlayne road, nw10 3jj. between mostyn gardens and mortimer road
bakerloo : kensal green
020 8969 9446 www.scarletandviolet.co.uk
mon - sat 9a - 6.30p

opened in 2006. owner: victoria brotherson
all major credit cards accepted
gift baskets. telephone orders. delivery in central london

kensal green > **s37**

Scarlet & Violet has a particularly English, endlessly seductive, shabby-chic charm. In December the flowers were all whisperers, beckoning me closer, no shouters here. The antique roses were the colours of fading love letters, the hyacynths all dusty pinks and pure white. Everything is for sale, the vases and china too. It all feels like a window on a world of ancient, arthritic butlers and eccentric copper plumbing. Here, the style is defined by loose, country-style flower arrangements, and if you can't get away to an old country house for the weekend, then try to get to *Scarlet & Violet*.

covet:
hyacynths planted in china teacups
anemones
antique roses
oversized milk jugs
candy-coloured hydrangeas in summer
tall enamel jugs
tulips
china teapots

story

emporium of indefinable beauty
4 wilkes street, e1 6qf. between hanbury and princelet streets
central / circle / hammersmith & city / metropolitan : liverpool street
020 7377 0313
mon - sat by appointment sun 1 - 5p

opened in 2000. owner: ann shore
all major credit cards accepted
customised individual items

spitalfields > s38

One of the best bits of advice Kaie gave me as I embarked on my *eat.shop* research was "look for the places that tell a story," and this is such a place. *Story* by name, story by nature. Last time I was there, I overheard a man exclaim, "It's like a cross between a shop and an art gallery." True, but so much more. *Story* is the expression of Ann's extraordinary sense of style. Her history in fashion, her work as a stylist and her ethical values all feed into a truly unique place filled with ethereal and practical beauty. It fills you with childish wonder as well, as do all the best stories.

covet:
customised dream catcher
tribal jewelery pieces
lime putty
sustainable cardboard boxes
glass droplets
lace cup tea light holder
individual pieces of clothing
liz clay hand felted collar

179

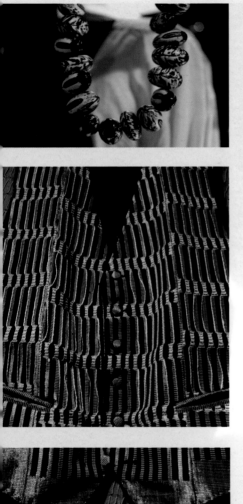

I think of waistcoats (vests in the US) as an escape from the sometimes drab uniformity of male fashion. Tailored to your measurements, the gorgeous waistcoats from *The African Waistcoat Company* are made from Nigerian hand-woven aso oke cloth, keeping alive a centuries-old African weaving tradition. I once wore a waistcoat as part of a theatre costume and I acquired a fan that wrote to me for months, bless him. It was the waistcoat, I tell you. They are super flattering. Or maybe it was the red wig. Guys, stick with Calum's waistcoats. They are spectacular.

covet:
waistcoats in authentic nigerian weaves,
  hand woven by yoruba craftsmen
jewelery from all over west africa
scarves in the aso oke cloth
antique nigerian:
  textile pieces
  robes
  stoles

the old curiosity shop

men's and women's shoe shop with big wow factor
13 - 14 portsmouth street   wc2a 2es. between sardinia and portugal streets
central / picadilly : holborn
020 7405 9891 www.curiosityuk.com
mon - sat 11a - 7p

opened in 1994. owner: daita kimura
mc. visa
custom orders

holborn > **s40**

I've had my shoe thing under control for a while now. Bags seem to be my current consumption issue. However, the experience of finding this wonderful building dating from 1567, immortalised by Dickens, now filled with the most gorgeous, quirky collection of footwear has set the shoe thing off again in me. My dreams are filled with elves cobbling on-site Daita's snub-toed creations, and I know it's only a matter of time until I find myself going back through this door. The thing is, I can't feel bad about it. Elves have to eat, too.

covet:
the old curiosity shop shoes made on-site
daita designed factory made shoes
megumi ochi
clickety click
george cox
takashi sugioka clothing
daydream nation clothing
k45 designed bags

twentytwentyone

20th and 21st-century design classics
18c river street, ec1r 1xn. between amwell street and myddelton square
northern : angel
020 7837 1900 www.twentytwentyone.com
mon - sat 9.30a - 5.30p

opened in 1996. owner: simon alderson
all major credit cards accepted
online shopping. registries. custom orders

islington > s41

Twentytwentyone has a small shop on Upper Street. But that's too easy. For the real fun, come to the showroom in a romantic courtyard off River Street. So (trust me here) turn left out of the Angel Tube station, carry straight on over the lights, turn right on Chadwell Street, cross Myddelton Square and you're there. This way you get to stroll through part of the Lloyd Baker Estate, an interesting bit of 19th-century London. The showroom itself is heaven, each object and piece of furniture revealing its beauty and why it's a classic, or will be.

covet:
lucienne day tea towels
sebastien wong convex mirror
barber osgerby home table
imbroglio calendar
alexander girard wooden dolls
eero saarinen grasshopper chair
marcel wanders fishnet chair
monkey boys random / non-random lights

two see

covent garden > **s42**

men's and women' s fashion-forward clothing
17 monmouth street, wc2h 9dd. between shaftesbury avenue and seven dials
piccadilly : covent garden <or> central : tottenham court road
020 7240 7692 www.twoseelife.com
mon - sat 11a - 6p sun 1 - 6p

opened in 2004. owners: dexter and terence wong
mc. visa
online shopping. occasional custom orders. gallery

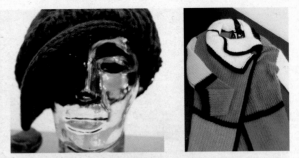

While I was at *Two See*, a boutique fashion nexus featuring pieces that range from bold and avant garde to eminently wearable, I was intrigued to watch regulars enter the place and efficiently scan the new merchandise. They seemed to know exactly what they wanted, and knew that they might find it here. I was a bit jealous, as I'm a shopping drifter. I go into a clothes shop for a white shirt and come out with a green dress every time. It's a blessing and a curse. In *Two See* I feel certain it would be a blessing.

covet:
dexter wong
patrick rzepski
hannah martin
jean-pierre braganza
emilio de la morena
pm
preen
david bradley

187

unto this last

modern and affordable design classics
230 brick lane, e2 7eb. corner of shacklewell street
northern : old street <or>
central / circle / hammersmith & city / metropolitan : liverpool street
020 7613 0882 www.untothislast.co.uk
mon - sun 10a - 6p

opened in 2000. owner: olivier geoffroy
all major credit cards accepted
custom orders

brick lane > s43

"Unto This Last" is the title of an essay written in 1860 by John Ruskin. Ruskin himself took the phrase from the parable of the vineyard labourers in Matthew's gospel. Why am I telling you this? Well, there's an ideology at work here at *Unto This Last*, the physical manifestation of which is micro-manufacturing. Olivier worked out the technological means to design furniture on a computer and cut it robotically in the back of the shop. That means locally made, affordable, made-to-size, beautiful pieces of state-of-the-art furniture. For us all. *Vorsprung durch technik*.

covet:
unto this last:
    spaceage cd / dvd wall rack
    solid ply table
    facet chair
    bedside cabinet
    coatstand
    polypropylene sphere lamp
    fruit bowl

victim

eclectic fashion

33 marshall street, w1f 7ex. between ganton street and foubert's place
bakerloo / central / victoria : oxford circus
020 7494 4044 www.victimfashionst.com
mon - sat 11.30a - 6.30p

opened in 2007. owner: mei-hui liu
mc. visa

soho > s44

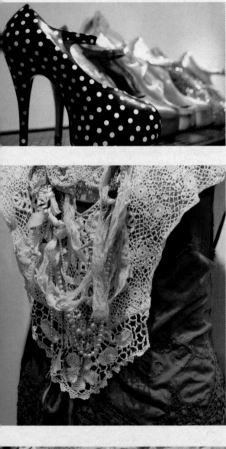

Mei-hui is never going to produce work clothes for the investment banker to wear to work. Well, never say never. Maybe on Dress-Up Friday? At *Victim* this season, there's a restructured, old-fashioned girl thing going down with a touch of '80s Madonna thrown in for good measure—for a romantic "like-a-virgin" party dress, look no further. Next season, who knows? This Korean-born designer is a precocious talent, that's for sure, and has made the transition from the east end to the big time in Soho with aplomb. Go girl.

covet:
dresses festooned with antique lace &
  strings of pearls
asymmetrical hems & lace trimmed skirts
quirky one-off jewelery
natacha marro shoes
alpha omega shoes

the eat.shop guides were created by kaie wellman and are published by cabazon books
for more information about the series, or to buy print or online books, please visit: eatsshopguides.com
the eat.shop guides are distributed by independent publishers group: www.ipgbook.com

eat.shop london was written, researched and photographed by caroline loncq
editing: kaie wellman   copy editing: lynn king   fact checking: emily mattson
map and layout production: julia dickey

my thanks go to simon, my *eat.shop* widower for the last three months, and jonjo for coming with me
sometimes, and for understanding the rest of the time. for their knowledge of the treasures of the shop
world i have to thank. jo, daisy, tina, mary and blake. the foodies deserve their special thanks also—the
amateurs: matty, al the fire, oz, saskia, louise and tom; and the pros: hege, magga, rogerio, fish and spike.
plus the miscellaneous: rod and thank you to the owners of the businesses i chose for being so unfailingly
helpful and accomodating.

cabazon books: eat.shop london   ISBN-13 978-0-9799557-0-9   copyright 2008 © cabazon books

every effort has been made to ensure the accuracy of the information in this book. however, certain details
are subject to change. please remember when using the guides that hours alter seasonally and sometimes
sadly, businesses close—check the businesses website beforehand or call for updated information on
opening and closing. the pictures and descriptions of each business are representational. please don't be
distraught when the business no longer carries or is not serving something you saw or read about in the
guide. all the businesses featured in this book are locally owned. this is not an advertorial guide, businesses do not pay to be featured.

the publisher cannot accept responsibility for any consequences arising from the use of this book